D1190615

The
Common Sense
Way to
Stock Market
Profits

Books by Claude N. Rosenberg, Jr.

Stock Market Primer

The Common Sense Way to Stock Market Profits

The Common Sense Way to Stock Market Profits

Claude N. Rosenberg, Jr.

The New American Library

To the apples of my eye,
wonderful Linda and Doug;
and to Elza and Claude,
who, after all,
really made it all possible.

Ralph Waldo Emerson once stated that:
"Nothing astonishes men so much as
common sense and plain dealing."

And Voltaire reflected that:
"Common sense is not so common."

With synthesis and added thought:
It is astonishing how productive
plain common sense can be.

Contents

Part Two: Protecting Yourself Against
Costly Mistakes in the Market

Part Three: Establishing a Profitable
Relationship with Your Stockbroker

Part Four: Conclusions

From Writer to Reader

If I were *you*, the prospective reader of this book, I would certainly want at least a few basic questions answered *before* I went any further. Perhaps the two most important of these would be:

1. What can the book do for *me?*

and

2. How does it differ from countless other works on the same subject?

The answers, in a nutshell, are that the book will teach you how to make big profits in the stock market—through a method which is both completely practical and understandable.

Admittedly, this is quite a claim—especially for a subject matter which is normally filled with hedged predictions and complex formulas. But the fact is that the vast majority of people make investing far more complicated than it really is. You see, the path to success in buying and selling securities is like so many other things we encounter in life in that the key is really the application of a great deal of *common sense*.

Call it logic. Call it sound reasoning. Call it proper thought process. Call it correct philosophy. In looking back over my dozen years in this business of making people's money grow, I can see how the common sense approach—and not a lot of complicated gobbledygook—has led to consistent success.

Thus, the goal of this book is to teach you to think and act correctly and to utilize a unique logic which has come as a result of many years of experience and untold hours of study and reflection.

To be specific, your reading will provide you with both a solid defense and a potent offense for your investing. The defense comes from giving you valuable advice which will keep you from making costly mistakes in the market. For example, everyone should understand the fads which take over the market constantly and should know how to avoid the fad investments. Furthermore, you should be schooled to know when the odds are stacked against you in certain stocks —and you should certainly be aware of the pitfalls of many brokerage companies' reports. In essence, the defense part of the book takes you into the "inner sanctum" of the investment world—something from which you are bound to come out far more sophisticated and knowledgeable.

The most important segment of the book—the offense—is devoted to the ultimate: achieving large profits while taking minimum risks. In reaching these crucial goals, you are given far more than just the right philosophies. You have actual tools you can put to work today to make your money grow. The book contains twenty-eight "Profit-Aids," which include an Industry-Rating Guide, a proper procedure for determining when to *sell* stocks, an approach to distinguishing attractive from unattractive issues, a Timing Guide which shows what price to pay for intended purchases, a guide to the correct buying of convertible securities, and other completely practical aids to set you on the road to success in the market. In addition, there is a very worthwhile discussion on how to amass large amounts of capital and even a method of solving that delicate problem of choosing the right broker and working correctly with him.

All in all, you will find what you read understandable and sensible and useful. It is my belief that you will come away with more "meat"—more applicable knowledge about stock investing—and that your performance right now (and over the years) will be greatly improved because of it.

One Necessary Definition

I just stated that you will find what you read understandable and that the successful approach to investing need *not* be complicated. Because of this, there is no need for you, the reader, to have any prior training, special skills, or broad knowledge of investing in securities. In short, the book will provide you with all you really need to know to succeed handsomely.

To obtain the maximum from what is to follow, you should, however, understand one basic term: the *Price-Earnings Ratio,* or, as it is more commonly called, the Price-Earnings *Multiple.* This section is included for those who are not yet familiar with this term. Its understanding is very simple and my definition follows.

Price-Earnings Ratio or Multiple

When you come right down to it, stock prices are but a function of two elements:

1. The earnings of the company itself.
2. What people are willing to pay for these earnings.

The first part (which can be called *profit* or *net income* as well as *earnings*) requires no skill on your part. They (the earnings, that is) are reported to you by the company involved on a *per-share basis,* and the only requirement is that you have a good idea as to where these figures are going from here. Are they likely to be sharply higher in the time ahead or are

they destined to drop—and in each case, to about what degree?

The second part (what price people might be willing to
pay for these earnings) does require judgment and knowledge
from you—something which should be well developed *after*
you have read the chapters which follow. Since I will refer
to Price-Earnings Multiple (let's abbreviate it as *P/E*) in a
number of chapters, we should have the definition clear—so
here we go!

The P/E reflects what people are willing to pay for earnings, and it is figured this way: *Market Price of the Stock ÷
Earnings Per Share = P/E.*

To illustrate, Company A's stock sells for $10 and it is
currently earning $1.00 per share. Its *P/E* is 10 ($10 ÷
$1.00 = 10), or, as they say in the investment business, "The
stock is selling for ten times earnings."

Now suppose the same Company A, with earnings per
share of $1.00, is selling for $20, not $10. What is the P/E?

The answer, of course, is: *20* ($20 market price ÷ $1.00
earnings per share = 20).

It is obvious that you would prefer to buy Company A at
$10 instead of $20, which is simply a way of saying that *the
lower the P/E the better.* You get more value in the way of
current earnings by paying ten times earnings than by paying
twenty!

Stated another way, the P/E shows you how many years
you will have to wait to have your purchase price earned by
the company involved *if there is no change in its profits in
the future.* If Company A continues to earn $1.00 per share,
it will take you ten years to have your $10 market price
earned for you, and naturally it is better to wait only ten
years than to wait twenty—which would be the case if you
paid $20 for the same stock (at a P/E of 20).

Needless to say, chances are one thousand to one that Company A will *not* earn the same dollars year after year. It will
earn way more in some years, way less in others, or perhaps
it is a growth outfit which might show consistent increases
as time goes by.

Most important, it is essential (although no doubt unnecessary) to point out that *a person should be willing to pay a P/E today based on just what kind of trend in earnings might be anticipated for the future.* If Company A's profits soar to $2.00 per share and then $3.00 and upward, you should be willing to pay a much higher price for the stock than if the $1.00 profits are to remain static or go downhill. Using our new terminology, you should be willing to pay a higher P/E for the growth company as opposed to the nongrowth.

By the same token, you should be ready to pay a higher P/E for Company A growing at a rapid clip than for Company B, which might not have the same favorable prospects.

Thus, *the P/E should be related to what the future holds.* But since no one has a completely clear crystal ball, the P/E is bound to be no more than what people *think* lies ahead. Thus, sentiments and emotions and all sorts of analytical and nonanalytical assessments get involved.

As mentioned, judgment is going to be required in arriving at the "right" P/E to pay for all stocks, and the ensuing pages will give you the perspective and thinking so that you will carry this all-important judgment factor with you the rest of your investing life.

The
Common Sense
Way to
Stock Market
Profits

Part One

Making Money
in the
Stock Market

Chapter One

Looking Ahead

Honesty, integrity, intelligence.

Compassion, perseverance, ambition.

These are all traits which help to make a man great. You could add more to this list, as could I, but I wonder whether you would think to add one of the most important of all. . . .

Foresight

The world's greatest leaders, teachers, scientists, and industrialists all possess this important quality. What good is the highway engineer who plans a two-lane road to handle today's traffic, only to find that by the time the road is built the two lanes are jammed and overcrowded? What good is the retailer who loads his shelves with sack dresses which will be out of style in a few months?

The answers are obvious, as is the answer to the following question: What good is the security analyst or investor who puts his money into situations which will be outmoded before long?

3

In short, such a person is only asking for trouble. The person who invests in "two-lane-highway" or "sack-dress" stocks will surely see his capital shrink. And since the object of this book is to show you how to make your capital grow, not shrink, we might as well start right here and emphasize what I consider to be one of the cardinal rules of investing. This rule, which constitutes Profit-Aid 1, is: *Always—but always—consider what lies* ahead *for the industry and company in which you have your money. And always realize that the smart money in the stock market is doing the same thing.*

Shrewd investors do not wait for an event to take place to invest their dollars; they anticipate the event and make their investment *before* the investing public realizes what is to occur.

Let me give you some examples of this procedure—examples of what foresight can mean in the stock market and how it can be utilized by you. Before doing this, let me apologize now for using personal examples, many of which point up successful experiences I have encountered in the stock market. They are not presented in an attempt to associate clairvoyance with the author; instead, they are used because they represent practical illustrations of theory. And since this work emphasizes the practical and the logical (as opposed to complicated "gobbledygook" theory so often advanced in books on stock investing), all that is presented is done with a sincere and legitimate intent.

The first instance which comes to mind is that of Zenith Radio. As far back as 1958 I was optimistic about the eventual success of color television in this country. To me it was an absolute certainty that we would at some time in the near future witness a revolution in the changeover from black-and-white to color TV. In the years 1958–1960 I was busy instructing numerous adult classes on "Investing and the Stock Market." And in each class I posed this thesis of mine that a stock like Zenith offered unusual potential because, among other things, the company would someday benefit from the "color revolution." Interestingly enough, I seldom found agreement with my idea. There were simply too many arguments against it. "The system of color broadcasting and receiving is not perfected and may never be," one person argued. True, indeed. The system was not yet perfect, but have you ever seen what movies, autos, airplanes, etc., looked like at their outset? I found it inconceivable that we would soon be sending space ships to the moon and exploring outer space and that we could not conquer something like color TV. "The sets are too expensive," another proposed. Also true, but the history of manufacturing is one of high price at the beginning when low volume prevails, then lower price as volume improves, and finally economical pricing when high volume exists.

I expected discussion and disagreement. Any person looking ahead must expect it. After all, if there were no such arguments, then the occurrence (in this case, color television) would be a reality, and the stocks of TV manufacturers would already have risen in price. In this case, the fact that color was not a reality gave TV stocks like Zenith little glamour in the eyes of the public. For this reason, Zenith could be purchased at bargain prices—as evidenced by the fact that its stock appreciated about eight times in the short period from 1958 to 1961. To carry this illustration one step further, I should point out that the high on Zenith stock for a number of years occurred in November of 1961—the very month that the company first brought color TV to market. In other words, there had been certain farsighted investors who had anticipated the enthusiasm which would obviously take place when Zenith entered the color market; these investors had the foresight to recognize what would happen well before it did; they bought the stock at very low prices when few people were thinking about this important development. Then, when the eventuality became a reality, they sold their stock, realizing that the existing price for Zenith stock was very high in relation to earnings and that it was therefore now anticipating the increased profits which would result in the near future for the company.

The Zenith story is just one of many proving how important it is to use foresight when buying stocks. Now let me give you two more examples which should prove meaningful and helpful to you in your quest to become a successful investor.

One of the best illustrations of how foresight can make you money and then how it can, in the same stock, save you from losing it right back involves the bowling issues, Brunswick and American Machine and Foundry. At about the same time that I became interested in Zenith Radio I was also attracted to Brunswick and AMF. It was obvious to me that every bowling alley in this country would have to be converted to automatic pinsetters and that Brunswick and AMF could benefit greatly from both this conversion and from the building of new alleys. With this in mind I recommended these stocks, particularly Brunswick, to certain investors who were looking for "special-situation" stocks in the market. In each case, I was trying to use foresight and look ahead to fantastic earnings, which I felt these companies would generate in the near future. But, at the same time that I was looking ahead, I could also see a strong and definite negative for this industry. There was no doubt in my mind whatsoever that the pinsetter market would eventually come to a rapid halt. I believed this for two reasons: first, because there were a given number of alleys in the country to be converted and once this was achieved the pinsetter manufacturers would have to look to the construction of *new* alleys for their business—and I knew that this would be a completely different market from that of the conversion market; and second, because I figured the market for bowling alleys in general would become saturated (after all, there is a certain amount of "fad" to bowling and you could not hope for a large building program to continue unabated) and this would, too, create great problems for Brunswick and AMF.

I never suggested either of these stocks without explaining my philosophy fully. I told my clients that these stocks looked to have dynamic possibilities because of the big demand which would be building up, but I also cautioned that these stocks would someday have to be sold because of the eventual saturation—*and that a person should never wait for this fear to become a reality*. I stated emphatically that these stocks were not like American Telephone, IBM, or other issues which might be placed in the safe-deposit box to hold forever. Instead, they were stocks with a great near-term story, which would have to be liquidated before the public became fearful of the saturation and before the saturation turned up in the form of lower earnings.

The rise in Brunswick and AMF was spectacular. Brunswick rose from a low of 2⅝ in 1957 to a high of 74⅞ in early 1961. In this latter year, the surface picture for this company was as rosy as could be. Backlogs and projections were fantastic. But, as mentioned, this was the surface picture. And, of course, the wise investor does not accept the surface picture as the gospel. The wise investor—the one who utilizes foresight as one of his strongest weapons—was questioning the future. He was looking past all the optimistic projections and was asking himself: "How soon will they reach the saturation point?" Industry statistics would have shown him that the conversion picture had been about completed and that the future for these pinsetters now rested with the building of new alleys. Such new construction could obviously not go on forever; thus, while the existing backlogs promised big business for the next year or so, the main question involved what was to happen to business after that. To support this negative approach further, all one had to do was to check on the profitability of the alleys themselves. Whereas a few years back, practically all bowling-alley owners were making good money, there suddenly came evidence that this rosy outlook was fading. Ownership of bowling alleys had suddenly become a precarious business—which naturally meant that new construction would come to a screeching halt before long.

All of this thinking became reality. By the time late 1961 and 1962 rolled around, many bowling-alley operators were in trouble and were not making money. The interesting thing is that the earnings of Brunswick and AMF did not begin to tail off *until 1962*. Yet Brunswick and AMF stock reached their highest points *a full year earlier—in 1961*. By the beginning of 1962, Brunswick had dropped from its 1961 high of about $75 per share to $46, and AMF plummeted from its peak of $60 to $36. And this isn't the end of the story. By January of 1963, both Brunswick and AMF were selling around $20 per share, and a year later the former was a measley $11, while the latter was around $18.

You can see, therefore, the importance of anticipating the future and not waiting for bad news to develop. The wisest investors in these bowling issues were those who did anticipate and who sold when the public was most convinced of bowling's great future. These shrewd investors peered "over the mountain" and saw the risks which loomed on the other side. They received these high prices because they had the fortitude to sell *before* any hint of danger became publicized. Naturally, they would have had to be just plain lucky to sell near the high; they may have sold at $40 or $50 either on the way up or as it commenced dropping. But $40 or $50 is a darn sight better than $20 or $10—a level to which the far-sighted investor would never have held.

A similar rags-to-riches and then back-to-rags (not really) story exists in another popular stock of the early 1960's— American Photocopy Equipment. I was fortunate enough to become greatly enthused about Apeco in its earliest stages, from which the stock soared over twenty times in but three to four years. But this is not the reason for my bringing up the Apeco story. My reason for doing so once again involves having the ability to look ahead and foresee trouble and, more important, to take action and sell accordingly before the trouble actually arrives.

The Apeco situation was somewhat different from that of the bowling issues. Whereas I stated that I warned investors from the very start that Brunswick and AMF would have to be sold at some time in the not-too-distant future, I honestly believed at the outset that Apeco was a stock which could be held forever. After all, the photocopy business was not a fad of any sort, and the replacement demand for photocopy paper (a very profitable part of this business) was something which would continue to grow in the future.

Flexibility, however, is an important attribute in investing.

The market has no place for a bullheaded "hear-no-evil, see-no-evil" person. In this case, the Apeco situation made as sharp a turnabout as did the bowling issues. Some of the reasons for the reversal could be foreseen. For one thing, too many new entrants had penetrated the photocopy scene. Eastman Kodak and Minnesota Mining entered the business somewhat early in the going, but by 1961 there existed a multitude of smaller companies, as well as some larger corporations, which were joining the swim. Secondly, the technology of photocopying was changing. The wet process was being replaced by the neater dry method, and then Xerox entered the field with its fabulous 914 Office Copier, which reprinted on *regular paper*. The whole replacement-demand business for photocopy paper had already changed completely, with the larger paper companies competing hard with the machine makers for this segment of the business. And the possibility of regular paper replacing the specialized photocopy paper loomed as a further threat to this very lucrative portion of the business.

Other internal problems loomed in particular at Apeco, and it was the basic change in the overall operating picture which forced me to change my mind about this stock. I cast aside my original love for Apeco and found that an objective appraisal of the future for this company was anything but rosy and was fraught with risks. All I can say is that my "Hold" recommendation on Apeco stock changed to a strong "Sell." In April of 1962 my last client was out of this stock at the price of $26 per share. This $26 price was still fifteen times their original purchase cost of around $1.75 per share, so no one was complaining. The important thing, however, is that Apeco stock slumped sharply after this, and in January of 1963 had fallen to around $11 per share and further to $7–8 a year later (and around this price in 1967). Once again, the willingness to look ahead and act before the reversal ever took place saved countless dollars.

Conclusions and an extension of Profit-Aid 1: The examples shown above are used for a reason. There is no desire to "toot one's horn" or imply that I always sell at or near the top or buy at or near the bottom. The important thing is that these illustrations are true to life. They represent actualities, not just theory. And they are typical of so many, many stocks in which anticipation of the future paid off, either in buying early before a large rise occurred or in selling before a large decline took place. The main thing is for you to school yourself to this way of thinking.

As I mentioned in our foreword, "From Writer to Reader," this book is devoted to making you more proficient, productive, and just plain profitable in your investments. To accomplish this, we will be discussing both the buying *and* selling of securities. This does not mean that I advocate a lot of activity by investors in buying and selling stocks; as a matter of fact, I am strongly opposed to excessive trading (it is the broker, not the investor, who benefits from this approach). It must be obvious, however, that holding stocks without the thought of *ever* selling is shortsighted. One of the common (and legitimate) criticisms of brokers and advisors is that "They never tell us when to sell," something which is covered in this first chapter and which is faced up to over and over from here on out.

Back to the subject of foresight and its utilization by you, we should now take the important step (which will be emphasized throughout the book) of *practicing what has been preached*. So now we go to the *method*, so that you can commence *now* to guide your investments correctly.

To succeed to the fullest, it is essential that you develop yourself as a "conceptual thinker." You must commence thinking (and acting) like those who prospered from the colossal Zenith-color-TV bandwagon and from Brunswick's and Apeco's—or like those who envisioned the dramatic changes which took place in the profitability of the airlines or a number of other growth-area discoveries.

But how? How can I literally force you into this profitable conceptual approach?

Just to repeat something else stated in our foreword, this book will supply you with the philosophies, the approaches, *and the tools* so necessary to excel in the stock market. Thus far, our discussion has centered around philosophy and approach, but now we come to the first real tool—which is really no more than an extension of the thought pattern of our Profit-Aid 1.

In presenting this tool, which is Profit-Aid 2, the goal is to set you thinking along *industry* lines; that is, to have you realize how important it is to have your money in the right *industries*—and then to show you what question marks apparently exist today about the future for these groups. In assessing these question marks, you are bound to spot a number of areas which are being downgraded unreasonably at this time —i.e., where you believe the negatives are far overshadowed by the positives. Wherever this be the case, you may be conscious of a concept which will lead to dramatic profits over the years for you.

Thus, Profit-Aid 2 will provide you with a rundown of the basic industries available in the marketplace, along with a summary of some of the more important positives and negatives applicable to their future. As such, it is bound to be a real aid to your own foresight. At the same time, Profit-Aid 2 provides you with a rough Glamour Rating of these industries at the time of this writing (late 1967). These Glamour Ratings are divided into five segments, with those enjoying the greatest acceptance by investors today given a 5 and those currently lodging in the investors' doghouse getting a mere 1. Needless to say, those with a 5 or a 4 had better not have serious negatives; if so, these should be classified as excellent sale candidates. Those which carry only 1 or 2 or even 3 should be assessed seriously, too, since the ability to overcome the problems they face will lead to a higher rating— which simply means a higher price-earnings ratio and correspondingly higher stock prices.

One warning should be given, however. There will be a natural tendency for you to look for the "sleepers" resting in the 1, 2, and 3 categories. This is fine—but only to a point. Every portfolio should start with a strong base, and this foundation should emphasize high-quality stocks which have clearly defined prospects for the future (most of which will be found in categories 4 and 5).

On the other hand, some careful thought can produce spectacular results, and I believe that our Profit-Aid 2—which is an Industry-Rating Guide—is an excellent "starting block" for those of you who are seeking something unusual in your investments. Actually, to make the job simpler, I have concluded Profit-Aid 2 with my broad thoughts on what might be undervalued and what appears to be overvalued to-day.

Rather than present the long list of industries and their plus-and-minus arguments here, I think it best to place this Aid as an appendix—at the end of the book. Many of the chapters to follow will give us other tools and approaches which will be pertinent to utilizing this Aid to better advantage. Therefore, we will find the "cart" *behind* the "horse," on page 212.

Chapter Two

Profits from Predicting
Pendulum Patterns

While it may seem far-fetched to relate pendulums to the stock market, I see two distinct similarities which I believe will be ever so helpful to you in your quest for profits from stocks.

The first of these analogies is really the result of human emotions. The fact is that we, as human beings, are prone to go to extremes in our thinking. Just as a pendulum swings from far left all the way back to far right and then back again, investors have a tendency to feel complete pessimism toward certain industries or certain individual stocks, only to change their opinions in time and swing over to an equally forceful optimism, only to revert again to the negative, etc. Naturally this pendulum motion is not the case in all industries or in all individual stocks. There are many, many areas for investment which do not go through this back-and-forth movement. But there are just as many areas which witness such performance rather consistently over the years, and I believe your understanding of these typical pendulum swings

13

will place you in an excellent position to profit from them.

There are so many groups in the market which make ideal examples. The steels, the cements, rubber stocks, railroads, aircraft manufacturers, and the airlines are but a half-dozen "model" cases. Over the post-World War II period these industry groups have "yo-yoed" in the fickle minds of investors on numerous occasions, traveling up and down from the apex of great confidence and glowing outlook to the nadir of pessimism and gloom and then back again. In some cases, this up-and-down movement is the result of some real fundamental changes which have taken place within the group; in other cases, the swing is caused only by the imagination and emotions of investors themselves. The airlines qualify as typical of the former; I will single out Crown Zellerbach as being typical of the latter. Your understanding of these two pendulum situations will enable you to approach stock investing in a far more sophisticated vein.

The airlines have followed pretty much of a feast-or-famine path in their operations. For a number of years they made big money, only to incur the wrath of the Civil Aeronautics Board, which insisted on more competition along the routes. Then the companies faced the jet age and found that the greatly enlarged capacity of the new planes (and their corresponding overhead) created profit problems—until demand caught up with supply and the companies prospered handsomely from their equipment expenditures. In the meantime, the airlines experienced normal fluctuations, in which traffic gains were strong when general economic conditions were favorable and naturally slowed in pace when the business climate was below par.

To achieve maximum profits in airline stocks, therefore, one really had to be flexible. He had to understand the pendulum swings of the industry; he had to anticipate these ups and downs and react accordingly, always endeavoring to be ahead of the crowd (he had to utilize foresight, as stressed in Chapter 1). Realizing this pattern, one might well have bought and sold airline issues three or four times over the post-World

War II period. And chances are that the future will follow a similar pattern. (For example, it is probable that the pressures from the regulatory authorities, the possible overordering of new equipment, and/or eventual transitional pains from the supersonic jets of the early 1970's will cause further up-and-down cycles from the group.)

Aside from the simple understanding of pendulum patterns, this first illustration should teach us another lesson: *that a person can become specialized and profit handsomely from knowing a pendulum group such as the airlines.*

Needless to say, we are living in an age of specialization, and the stock market is certainly no exception. While we would all prefer to buy into companies which are not going to suffer drastic ups and downs, we would only be ostrichlike if we stuck our heads in the sand and considered this approach the sole way of profiting in the market.

Later on I will discuss cyclical (sensitive to the business cycle) stocks rather fully, but for the moment I want to emphasize one piece of advice: *Get to know one or two typical yo-yo, pendulum industries and, once confident that you are somewhat of an expert, wait for the right swing movements and invest accordingly.*

While it is hardly realistic to think you will ever have the time to become expert on many fields, you should be able to develop expertise—and a sixth-sense type of market "feel"— on one or two groups. By placing a certain percent of your investable dollars in such specialized areas, your chances for success are greatly improved. This prospect might hold more glamour for you if you realize that many such pendulum swings will multiply your money significantly over the short period of a few years, thereby creating a very respectable rate of return on your dollars. Incidentally, our Industry-Rating Guide (Profit-Aid 2) should be helpful to you in the eventual choice of some specialized fields.

Pendulum swings similar to the airlines have occurred in numerous other industries in any and all periods of history— and they will be repeated in the future.

As mentioned, I will cite Crown Zellerbach as an example of pendulum swings in the market which can evolve even when drastic changes are *not* occurring in a given industry or company. Before going further, perhaps I had better clarify the word "change." Needless to say, change of some sort is inevitable in almost every situation, and thus we are referring to more-than-normal alterations in pattern.

The reason I have chosen Crown Zellerbach is that the 1959–1963 period was a pretty flat one for the company, with earnings at the end of the span almost identical to those at the beginning. Here are the exact earnings figures Crown reported:

Year	Earnings Per Share
1963	$2.50
1962	2.47
1961	2.33
1960	2.56
1959	2.51

A look at this record, which was no more than one of stability, might lead one to the conclusion that Crown stock was probably a very dull performer in the market over this period and that there was probably little fluctuation in its market price.

Such was *not* the case!

The fact is that Crown fluctuated no less than nine points in each one of the years illustrated and that in one year (1961) it did so by over twenty-two points. Since Crown's average market price was around $50 during these years, this means that it experienced a minimum eighteen-percent deviation up and down and a maximum of almost forty-five percent.

To be specific, the stock had the following high and low points for each of the years:

COMMON-STOCK PRICE RANGE

Year	High	Low
1963	60⅝	45
1962	59⅞	37½
1961	60⅝	46⅝
1960	49½	36⅛
1959	54⅞	45⅝

Shown another way, the stock had a wide divergence each year in the price-earnings multiple investors were willing to pay for it:

Year	High	Low
1963	24	18
1962	24	15
1961	26	20
1960	19	14
1959	22	18

The important consideration here is that the paper industry in general, and Crown Zellerbach in particular, really experienced, as mentioned, very little in the way of change over this span—and yet Crown stock had some significant market swings. The pros and cons on the industry were almost identical in each of the years; it was the human reaction to these pros and cons which caused this cold, then hot, then cold, then hot occurrence. Each year the stock experienced strong enough buying interest and sufficient selling pressure so as to cause wide fluctuations. In other words, every year found hope springing eternal (with high price-earnings ratios existing) and disappointment bringing gloom (and corresponding low P/E's).

The lesson to be learned is so very simple: *that it is seldom that something which is fundamentally one way now should do a complete turnabout and be exactly the opposite in a short period of time.* Things are seldom all black or all white; there are shades of gray in between. Thus, when investor psychology reacts so violently as to say only black or white, you should be alert to take advantage of the swings which result. In short, the potentials from pendulum movements are interesting, and you should be prepared to profit from them.

This brings us to Profit-Aid 3. After the previous discussion, it should be obvious that we might build ourselves into an interesting buying program by pinpointing those lower pendulum levels which apparently attract investment demand in certain securities. In our Crown Zellerbach illustration, the person who chose buying levels at around fifteen times earnings during 1960–1962 placed himself in a fine position. In each case, he would have had the opportunity to sell out at substantially higher prices during that very year—and it would have been his knowledge of Crown's pendulum pattern which would have accomplished this for him. As a matter of fact, this pattern alone would have saved him from having to be too analytical (he wouldn't have had to be an expert in the paper industry or the individual company) and he wouldn't have had to bother himself with the emotional task of assessing all the little problems which might have been cropping up for Crown during the year. Not all stocks, of course, lend themselves to this kind of behavior, but a goodly number do. I could list hundreds of stocks and show such patterns, but I think it best if I concentrate on those which have proved themselves to me over the years. Since this is a publication which will not be revised monthly, I will highlight companies which are not subject to very erratic earnings. In other words, I prefer to center my focus on companies which have shown some consistency in profit progress—but which still seem to experience pendulum swings in their stock prices during almost every year.

All you need do, therefore, to benefit from Profit-Aid 3 is to approximate earnings for the year, multiply these earnings by the multiple I will indicate as the pendulum buying point, and place your buying order accordingly. For example, I have found Standard Oil of California to be consistently attractive when it reaches about 10½ times estimated current earnings. If the 1967 estimate for the company is $5.30 per share, then I should set my sights at 10½ times $5.30, or at around $55.50. Apparently, investment managers and/or the public are just plain attracted to this stock at these levels, and I might as well benefit from this pattern.

The case of Standard of California is not terribly exciting, as the stock is not viewed as a dramatic-growth vehicle and it does not normally have very violent swings. Perhaps a better illustration (with more profit potential) would be Chas. Pfizer & Co., the fine drug-chemical company. This stock seems to attract investment support at a higher figure than Standard—at around twenty times earnings. If you look at the past record of Pfizer you will see that purchases made at about twenty times earnings have proved quite propitious. And in practically every year! Our most recent full year (1966) proved this to be the case once again. In May of 1966, the stock dropped to $60; with profits for that year expected to be over $3.00 per share, this meant that a P/E of twenty existed. Now that might seem high to the casual observer, but it has not been for Pfizer (whose earnings have been quite predictable). Within a few months, the stock was selling at the higher end of its normal pattern—at twenty-five times earnings, twenty-five-percent improvement. Thus, it was a pendulum swing—not any change in the company's future—which accounted for a profit-making opportunity.

Before presenting some specifics for you in this Profit-Aid 3, let me say that it is bound to be more useful and practical in what might be described as "normal" markets. A violent bear market may negate the patterns, but then such markets are very much the exception; static-to-strong markets exist (fortunately) in the vast majority of years.

Following are some pendulum-pattern favorites of mine. I have included approximate buying and selling multiples for all the stocks, even though I do not suggest your being so active as to try to both buy and sell in any year. I would prefer to see you buy a stock such as Bristol-Myers "right" and hold it, even after it has gone to its pendulum swing upward

—so long as the company is growing consistently and at a rapid rate. In other words, I am not advocating trading activity on your part; as mentioned, I am opposed to this, and my Profit-Aid 3 is more intended as a buying guideline for some fine companies than as a trading "whirl."

PROFIT-AID 3: PENDULUM-PATTERN STOCKS

Company	Attractive Pendulum Buying Range	"Normal" Resistance Pendulum Selling Area
Bristol-Myers	30 times	40 times
Borden	15	20
General Electric	20	25
Hewlett-Packard	25	40
IBM	35	45
Litton Industries	25	35
Pfizer	20	25
Simplicity Pattern	15	20
Standard Oil of Calif.	10½	13
Texaco	13	16

Why Do Some Stocks Go Down When the News Gets Good? We come now to another type of pendulum pattern which I feel is essential for you to learn. To understand this pendulum, which incidentally will give you a truly sophisticated approach to stock investing, it is important to realize how and why *big* money is made in the stock market in so-called "special situations." As I see it, there are basically three logical approaches to making money in the market, namely:

1. Buying already recognized (blue-chip type) stocks and "sitting" on them for a period of years.
2. Buying cyclical stocks when they are depressed and selling them when they have been inflated by an upturn in their cycle.
3. Buying stocks in little-known (or at least not generally popular) companies and holding them for some future developments which you believe will bring them more

into the public limelight and which will hike their market prices substantially.

The last approach is what we in the investment business term "special situations." And how very profitable this effort can be!

Actually, the major prerequisite for finding successful special-situation stocks is the foresight I dwelled on in Chapter 1. The fabulous profits made in Zenith, Brunswick, Apeco, and others were all based on the ability to look ahead—the ability to spot an optimistic development before it was recognized by the investing public. In the case of Brunswick and Apeco, this foresight was necessary on two ends: first, to anticipate the upcoming events which would improve earnings and, second, to recognize some looming negatives and sell before they were understood.

I should point out that not all special-situation stocks have such negatives; indeed, many are fundamentally secure companies which can continue growing almost indefinitely and which, like in the blue-chip approach, might be held forever.

I think it is fair to say, however, that the majority of stocks in this category are not indestructible. Which is just another way of saying that you as a buyer will someday have to become a seller to reap maximum rewards from your investment. In this majority, therefore, the shrewd investor realizes he will have to follow a pattern such as the following:

1. Buy before the industry or the company chosen is recognized for its real potential. The fact that the growth potential is not recognized generally means you will find some stocks very reasonably priced in the market.
2. Have patience and wait for the anticipated developments to take place, or at least for the public to become enamored with these prospects.
3. Sell when the stock prices reflect these possible developments.

The first two of these three rules for special-situation investment are obvious, but the third—and all-important—commandment brings about very strange market behavior. In a nutshell, it means that you will have to sell when opinions and forecasts are the rosiest—which is a difficult technique to master. I feel confident you will master it, though—especially if you realize that the approach is just another pendulum-type pattern. Let's use the Zenith Radio example utilized in Chapter 1, because it will illustrate the foresight, the pendulum, the approach, etc.

When I first became interested in Zenith stock, it was anything but a public favorite. As a matter of fact, it was a neglected issue, as was the whole radio-television group. This neglect, of course, is always to the prospective buyer's great advantage, since it keeps the stock at a very reasonable price level relative to its earnings and dividends. In the case of Zenith, the stock was selling for a "dirt-cheap" seven times earnings and provided an above-average yield of five percent.

I have already commented on the type of reasoning which attracted me to Zenith at that time (1958). Management was outstanding, the company boasted a quality product with an efficient distribution system to back it up, and finances were exceptionally strong. Of great significance was the status of the television market in general. While statistics showed that most American families already owned a television set (meaning that the industry's saturation rate was high), it had been a number of years since the last TV-buying splurge by the public, and thus the replacement cycle was looming on the horizon. In addition, the acceptance of TV as an entertainment vehicle was creating good demand for second and third sets within a household ("The Three Stooges" for Junior, "Dance Party" for Susie, and an intellectual pursuit such as a good Western for Dad—all with the same viewing time). Of even greater importance, however, was the prospect for an entirely new market in the future for color TV. If color really clicked, it promised huge potentials. With over one hundred million black-and-white sets to be, hopefully, rendered obsolete, you can see what kind of prospects a company such as Zenith might enjoy in the future.

With these items in mind, Zenith stock looked to be at the far swing of a pendulum (the negative end), readying itself for an optimistic reversal.

Let me make it clear that the color possibilities were *not* imminent. But the wise investor knows if he waits for a trend to take place, he is going to be late. In this case, the investor should have known that Zenith in the midst of color prosperity was not going to be available at any reasonable price like seven times earnings.

The ensuing years were great ones for Zenith shareholders, as they benefited from the double-barreled effect of higher company earnings and a higher P/E multiple. But this is not the lesson at hand. So let's go on!

A few paragraphs back I brought out the all-important word "saturation." This is particularly important here, because the farsighted individual in our Zenith example should also have realized that the television business under ordinary circumstances—without a great replacement cycle and without a color revolution—was a very difficult one and one which would *not* command a high P/E in the market. In other words, the shrewd thinker should have conditioned himself to the idea that he would someday have to sell his Zenith stock.

But when? When should he plan to take his profit?

The ideal way of approaching this all-important question would have been (and should be) to follow three basic steps —which we should label as our Profit-Aid 4. Here they are:

1. Determine in your mind what a "normal" P/E should be for Zenith *after* the color revolution is in full swing, when the company will have no explosive "kickers" to its earnings any longer. Stated another way, determine what Zenith's P/E should be under normal operating conditions.
2. Forecast as closely as possible what Zenith might earn under these advanced conditions.
3. Multiply your future P/E times your guesstimate of future earnings—the result of which will be your future price to sell (or at least the price after which your appreciation potentials might become very limited).

Obviously all of this involves considerable guesswork. Who can really tell how big or small earnings might be in the future for a company? The answer is that you cannot! But, as time rolls on and your anticipated event (in this case, color TV) gets closer to fruition, you may be able to establish a pretty firm range from which you can work.

Your projection of a normal multiple is also inexact, but at least you can arrive at a number which puts you "in the ball-park."

The important thing at the beginning is not to pinpoint your selling price; this will come later. The crucial point to establish is that you are buying the stock "right."

In our 1958 Zenith example, an assessment of the multiple alone would have sufficed. If we just believed that this stock at some time in the future would sell at only twelve or thirteen times earnings, we would have had confidence buying it at only seven times. Then, without pinpointing any profit figure for the future—just assuming that the figures would be higher than at present—the stock would clearly have qualified as a strong "buy" for results that could clearly have looked to be sensational (after all, a future doubling of earnings and a corresponding doubling of the seven-times multiple would bring about a quadrupling of the stock's price).

But, again, when do we sell?

Let's assume we had figured on a doubling of both earnings and the P/E for Zenith. With this in mind, we would *not* have been tempted to sell until the stock hit $40, as follows:

Zenith stock in 1958: $9
Earnings expected (and realized by Zenith in that year): $1.37
P/E Ratio ($9 ÷ $1.37) = 6.6

Earnings expected for Zenith in future: $2.80
P/E anticipated at that time: 14
Market price expected in future ($2.80 × 14) = $40

The history of Zenith shows that the company increased its earnings by about fifty percent by 1961, even before it had benefited from color at all. From this it was obvious that our

$2.80-per-share profit figure for the future (with color) was too low. Thus, as part of our reassessment (Chapter 6 will emphasize the importance of reviewing statistics and objectives on a regular basis), we should resort to a new earnings figure. Since 1961's income figure was $1.99, we might have assumed a doubling of this, thereby raising our sights to $4.00.

How about our future "normal P/E" for Zenith? Should this, too, be altered? Probably so. Zenith's image in the investment community had improved considerably because of its superior operating results through a rather difficult period for most TV manufacturers. Considering this improved stature might have allowed us to increase our fourteen multiple to, say, eighteen (about equal to the average P/E on the Dow Jones Industrial Average).

So now our price objectives had improved from $40 per share for Zenith to $72, as follows:

Future Zenith earnings with color: $4.00
Future "normal" P/E: 18
Future price for Zenith stock ($4.00 × 18) = $72.00

Interestingly enough, Zenith stock rose to $82 in November of 1961—just when the company was *commencing* color production. At that time, however, Zenith earnings (as shown) were still in the $2.00-per-share area—not $4.00. In other words, Zenith stock had gone to an exorbitant *forty-one times earnings*.

Now—the emotional investor might have considered this forty-one times as normal. Our thinking said "No!" According to our reasoning, the public was now paying a price for Zenith stock which anticipated all the good news visible for some time.

The unsophisticated thinker would probably have rationalized the stock's high price by taking the following tack:

Zenith is selling at forty-one times earnings at present. This is a normal and reasonable multiple for the company —one which can be expected to exist in the future.

When color evolves, Zenith should eventually earn about $4.00 per share. Multiplying the forty-one figure times the $4.00 earnings will give us a $164 price for Zenith stock. This is the time to hold on to Zenith (if it is already held) or the time to buy it for future gains.

What a weak and foolish argument! This individual fails to realize that the stock market is always trying to anticipate what lies ahead and that by the time Zenith is toward the end of the color revolution the smart investors will be anticipating the competitive conditions which probably lie ahead for set manufacturers. In short, the smart thinker will recognize that Zenith will *not* deserve a forty-one-times multiple on a realistic, nonemotional basis. Thus, whereas the emotional individual is lulled into a false sense of security in looking at Zenith at $82, the trained investor recognizes that the cream is out of the stock for some time. The latter realizes that a good portion of the future good news is already discounted by the stock's market price.

So you can see again how pendulums can exist even in very fine companies (which Zenith certainly is) *even without* any large negatives existing.

Let me summarize by drawing this truly typical pendulum:

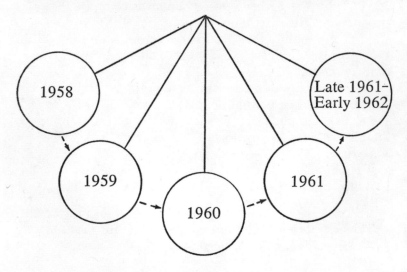

1958

Pendulum negative. Zenith stock at seven times earnings—stock not anticipating anything glamorous for the company.

1959

Pendulum swinging positive. Zenith stock reflecting higher current-earnings levels.

1960

Further positive swing. Zenith stock selling on basis of both rising earnings and higher P/E multiples.

1961

Enthusiasm by public for Zenith stock as it sells at higher and higher multiples.

Late 1961– Early 1962

Zenith at forty-one times is now anticipating much of future potential (our 18 "normal" multiple times our hoped-for $4-per-share earnings = $72, *less than the stock's current price*).

The wise investor, using this objective and realistic approach, could never have been enticed by Zenith at these high levels. Since $72 was his *longer-term* potential, he would have been a seller in the $60–$82 price area.

Needless to say, the vast majority of stock buyers have *not* been trained to think this way. They are guessing and guessing alone. And it is this guesswork I am trying to eliminate for you. Not that the stock market can be viewed as a science. But there is a method which breeds success, and this method is based on a sound and logical (common sense) approach, something which is not complicated and which you can master easily.

The Zenith example is hardly an isolated one: it is one of thousands. I urge you to read it over many times, because it typifies this correct method I am preaching.

Chapter Three

Product Differentiation— A Key to Success in the Stock Market

As the famous author Gertrude Stein, said, "Rose is a rose is a rose is a rose."

While, of course, Miss Stein did not mean to imply that one rose is exactly the same as the next, I would like to use the tone of this quotation in a way which will be helpful to you in your investments. You see, there are certain products in existence which vary little or none from one manufacturer to another. For example, there is obviously little or no difference between one bag of cement produced by Kaiser Cement or Ideal Cement or any other producer. Indeed:

Cement is a cement is a cement is a cement.
and . . .
Gypsum is a gypsum is a gypsum is a gypsum.
and . . .
Aluminum is an aluminum is an aluminum is an aluminum.

What I am saying is that these products are basically similar from one producer to another. Gypsum from U.S. Gypsum is the same as that from National Gypsum. And aluminum ingots from Alcoa are the same as those from Kaiser or Reynolds. I am hammering this point home for one important reason—because *whenever such product similarity exists, the basis for purchase by the product's users will depend on service and certain personal factors, but mainly it will depend on PRICE.* And, to my way of thinking, *industries which are free from price battles offer you as an investor an unusual advantage,* while those which are constantly subject to pricing wars are inherently weaker holdings.

Compare gypsum and cement, for example, with products like nylon and orlon. At the beginning, Du Pont possessed something completely unusual in these synthetic fibers—and it was this product differential which brought them a fat profit margin and many years of high earnings. As a matter of fact, the chemical industry serves as a good illustration of my thinking. Those companies which emphasize products which have individuality have done far better than those which produce ordinary "building-block" chemicals which are more easily manufactured by others and which carry no price stability.

This is not to say that money cannot be made in companies unless they have products of individual character. Sometimes unusual merchandising or marketing know-how or production know-how or geographical advantage can overcome the disadvantages of no-product-differential. The oil industry is a good example of this. Certainly oil is a nondifferentiated product: one barrel brought out of the ground by Texaco is basically the same as one barrel produced by Sunray DX. Yet, the management of one (Texaco) has built solid geographical diversification and an extra-efficient distribution and marketing system which has produced steadily rising profits over the years, whereas Sunray has been able to keep its net income only at about the same level and has been unable to exhibit any consistent growth.

The steel industry offers another good example. Despite product similarity, Inland Steel outperformed the industry for many years because it enjoyed a protected position in the heavily industrialized Chicago area. As more competition moves into this region, however, Inland will experience the effects of its nondifferentiated product and it will experience tougher sledding than in the past.

Many times you will find there is a vast difference in product loyalty and uniqueness within an industry. Consider the food field. Most people will agree that it is extremely difficult to distinguish between the various brands of salt or sugar. Chances are the housewife, in making out her shopping list, will simply write "salt" and "sugar" and not demand Brand A or Brand B. In contrast, when she is planning to buy spaghetti or mayonnaise she will usually have a definite choice. Whether it be Franco-American or Chef Boy-ar-dee spaghetti or Best Foods or Kraft mayonnaise, she will have a specific reason for the purchase, and price may not be the major consideration. For these reasons, I am sure you will not be surprised to know how much better Corn Products (the maker of Best Foods), National Dairy (Kraft), and Campbell Soup (Franco-American spaghetti) have done earnings-wise over a long period of time than typical salt or sugar companies. When you come right down to it, the consideration of product differentiation has reared its head again—and this is just one more illustration of its usefulness.

What I am saying, therefore, is that you as an investor need some outstanding feature in the company you are buying to give you any kind of decent performance in a non-differentiated-product industry. While you should always seek out well-managed enterprises regardless of industry, you have much more going for you at the beginning if you don't have to fight this disadvantage of no differentiation. This is one of the major reasons I have been bullish over the years about proprietary (nonprescription) drug stocks (more on this in Chapter 14). Most of the proprietary companies enjoy product uniqueness which gives them the ability to raise prices almost at will—and this leads to higher and higher profits as time goes on.

Thus, our Profit-Aid 5 encompasses the following dictum: *Give real weight in your stock selection to companies which possess differentiated products; and recognize that those with typical nondifferentiated products will need something unusual to overcome this disadvantage sufficiently so as to become consistent growth vehicles.*

Actually, the number of pure differentiated areas within our economy is really quite limited. Now, both to implant the idea of what constitutes differentiation and to lead you to specific fields which hold this attraction, I have compiled a short list for you. This is an extension of Profit-Aid 5 and it points up some paramount nondifferentiated areas, some typical companies engaged in the business at hand and a bit of reasoning as to just why the companies enjoy some uniqueness.

DIFFERENTIATED PRODUCT INDUSTRIES AND COMPANIES

Industry	Typical Company or Companies and Reasoning Behind Uniqueness	
Cosmetics	Chesebrough-Pond's	Major lines (Vaseline and Pond's) have strong public acceptance and shelf appeal, which give them unique character and firm price structure.
	Bristol-Myers	Just think of Clairol and relate above reasoning!
Soft Drinks	Coca-Cola, Pepsico, Seven-Up	How many household words are there as familiar as "Coke," "Pepsi," or "7-Up."
Proprietary Drugs	Practically all major companies, i.e., Bristol-Myers, Norwich, Plough, Sterling Drug, Warner-Lambert, Miles Laboratories, Johnson & Johnson, have individual products which fit the differentiated-product category.	
Office Equipment	IBM	To say nothing of the all-important computer acceptance, consider what the letters "IBM" mean on a typewriter.

DIFFERENTIATED PRODUCT INDUSTRIES AND COMPANIES

Industry	Typical Company or Companies and Reasoning Behind Uniqueness	
Services	American Express	Travelers Cheques and other travel services.
	Commerce Clearing House	Differentiated aid to lawyers, accountants, etc.
	Dun & Bradstreet	Accepted credit ratings.
Photography	Eastman Kodak	Film, cameras, and accessories.
	Polaroid	Instant picture-taking; film, cameras, accessories.
Automobiles	Chrysler, Ford, GM	Models do change, but they carry certain distinctions with them.
Construction Equipment	Caterpillar	This is a quality-reputation differentiation, but we all know what "Cat" means to equipment buyers.

In contrast, think how the above reasoning does not hold true for:

Copper and other metals
Building supplies (i.e., asphalt, lumber, plywood)
Container manufacturers
Paper, especially industrial type (consumer paper products can build a select following).

Naturally, you cannot distinguish all industries in this way. Pursuits such as banking, food chains, retail trade, and many others simply defy categorization. The main thing is for you to be conscious of the distinct advantages and disadvantages when you run across companies whose products fit directly into a niche of definitely having or lacking differentiation. Remember, you stand a better chance for success when a rose is *not* a rose is *not* a rose, etc. This awareness will help you separate the attractive from the unattractive company and will in turn separate the most-profitable from the least-attractive investment.

Chapter Four

What Price Growth?

I am sure I will encounter no argument when I state that it is extremely beneficial to investors to buy and own stocks of companies which will show consistent increases in earnings (*per share*) over the years. The theory behind buying so-called "growth companies" is virtually undisputed! The difference of opinion lies with the decision of what price a person should be willing to pay for growth.

Naturally, there is no single formula for answering this question: What price for what growth? I could make a strong argument to convince you that a range of ten to fifteen times earnings is ample for a five-percent-growth company, that fifteen to twenty times is suitable for a ten-percent-growth outfit, and that a progression upward of about an additional five in the multiple for each additional five percent of growth is justified. This mathematical thinking alone, however, would hardly provide you with the right market price for securities in general. There are too many other considerations which have to be thrown into the "hopper," not the least of which are institutional support (or lack of it), general market psychology, supply of stock available, and so-called "glamour image." Any one of these (and other) factors can alter your mathematical computation and lead you to a conclusion for either a higher or a lower price-earnings ratio than might seem justified by the figures alone.

Does all this mean that we should throw up our hands in despair and close our eyes to market-price evaluation? Of course not! We must base our selection and our timing on something, and the relationship between annual compound growth rates and P/E ratios as indicated in the second paragraph is as good a starting point as any.

Opponents of the growth theory of investing can, of course, throw cold water on the whole approach—by simply posing the question: "What happens if there is a reversal in public opinion and the P/E paid by investors for an individual stock, an industry group, or the market in general is lowered considerably?"

A good question, indeed! We certainly do not want to pay twenty times earnings today for a stock and find it selling at ten times earnings five years from now, *regardless of the company's growth rate in the interim.*

Or do we?

The fact is—*we may be willing to own a stock and see its P/E come down sharply, provided its rate-of-earnings growth is strong enough.* The mathematics of compounding figures are amazing; a little later on in this chapter I will show you just how amazing by proving to you that a stock like IBM can be a decent investment today at forty times earnings even if we visualize it selling at only twenty times earnings ten years hence.

Before we come to this and other illustrations which will prepare us better for determining what price we should pay for growth, we should explore and conclude just what constitutes a good investment.

Don't worry, I'm not going to bore you with a long philosophical dissertation on investments. What I am going to do is give you a simple explanation—one which will have a practical application for you.

All investments should be judged on the basis of *annual rate of return on invested capital.* Whether it be the ownership of raw land, income property, a private business, or the holding of securities, the important consideration is the average rate of return on the money invested. Naturally, this rate of return will have to include both the income received from the investment plus the appreciation (or minus the loss) on the investment over its life. Let me emphasize that you have to consider both the income and the increment in value (or loss) in arriving at the average annual rate of return. I do this because I have heard such abuses—even by very intelligent people—of what really constitutes a good rate of return. For example, I have heard people brag about investments which seemingly yield very high rates—where the owners have failed to account for the loss of capital if the investment were to be liquidated (i.e., a second mortgage). By the same token, I have heard individuals boast about the great investment they made buying that acre of Tibetan land, where their $1,000 investment in 1944 was just sold for $2,000. While a doubling of investment sounds glamorous, twenty-three years is a long time to wait for it, and, as a matter of fact, such performance amounts to a compounded rate of return of only about three percent per year. (Naturally, any taxes paid on the property should be accounted for, and this would reduce the return further.) At any rate, a mere bond would have achieved similar results, and certainly almost any conservative common-stock investment would have achieved far superior effects.

As far as the securities market is concerned, we should approach the problem of investing wisely, just as the professional advisors do. So now we come to Profit-Aid 6, *which shows us how to weigh the merits of bonds, preferred stocks, and common stocks by computing, as closely as possible, the probable rate of return on our invested capital over the years.* It is quite simple to do this when we are considering bond investments, and fairly easy to figure in the case of preferreds. For example, assume you are considering investment in a General Motors bond which pays $3.00 a year; the bond sells at $90.00 and it will mature in ten years at $100.00. Your average rate of return on this bond will be about 4.3 percent, figured as follows:

1. Paying $90 for a $3 yearly income provides a yield of 3.3 percent per year ($3 ÷ $90 = 3.3 percent).
2. Your $90 purchase will be worth $100 in ten years, for a gain of $1 a year, or slightly over 1 percent per year.
3. The 3.3 percent as shown in (1) plus the 1 percent as figured in (2) = 4.3 percent, which is the average rate of return per year.

As a potential investor, you will want to determine whether this 4.3 percent is attractive relative to other investments and make your decision accordingly.

The analysis of a preferred stock will be similar to the General Motors bond illustration, except that there is no maturity date or price you can count on. In essence, you should figure what the current yield amounts to and make your decision based almost solely on this.

In the more interesting area of common stocks, the approach is more complicated—but it can be so wonderfully rewarding that it is worth exploring. First of all, let's consider the case of a common stock where earnings are quite predictable, i.e., the case of a good electric-utility stock. Electric utilities in a growing area should represent good investments because their product (electricity) is in steadily growing demand. But this is a bold generalization to make—mainly because we have to consider what price we have to pay in the market for this "assured" growth and because we haven't even considered what our average rate of return on investment might be. If we have to pay too high a price and our return will be very low, perhaps we're better off placing the money elsewhere.

For example, let's look at Pacific Gas & Electric Company, or any number of a host of utilities whose earnings have grown—and should reasonably be expected to grow in the future—at four to five percent a year. Stocks such as these are selling in today's market at about fifteen times earnings, with a yield of four percent. Obviously this four-percent yield figure is *not* the total rate of return on your investment. Why? Because the company's earnings are expanding four to five percent a year! Assuming the stock sells at the same P/E a year, two years, or five years from now, the four-to-five-percent annual improvement in earnings will be directly reflected in appreciation of the stock's market price. Thus, this investment will return an average of eight to nine percent on your money (four-percent current yield plus four-to-five-percent earnings growth). To be specific, here is what happens when you buy XYZ utility today at $100 per share, when its earnings are $6.65 per share (P/E of fifteen) and its dividend is $4.00 (4-percent yield). One year from today, you look back on your investment, and here is what you find:

1. You have received $4.00 in dividends, which, based on your $100 investment, amounts to a return of 4 percent.
2. XYZ's earnings per share have advanced 5 percent, from $6.65 to about $7. XYZ stock is still selling at 15 times these latter earnings and is now 105 (15 × $7 = $105).
3. The five-point improvement from 100 to 105 amounts to a 5-percent appreciation.
4. The 4 percent shown in 1 plus the 5 percent in 3 gives you a total 9-percent rate of return in this one year.

This is the kind of thinking you should have done when you first considered XYZ. If you had, you would have compared this projected nine-percent rate of return with, for example, the 4.3 percent from the GM bond about which we talked and with other investment possibilities. The return on XYZ was about twice that of the GM bond, and you probably would have considered this sufficient reward for taking the risk that XYZ would either:

1. Not show a five-percent advance in net income; or
2. Not sell as high as fifteen times earnings in the future.

The exact line of reasoning prevails when considering any stock investment. Using utility stocks again as examples, you would weigh the purchase of a rapidly growing vehicle such as Florida Power and Light as follows:

1. FPL has averaged a ten-percent growth in earnings in recent years.
2. You will have to pay twenty times earnings for FPL stock, and the yield from same is a small two percent.
3. If the company's growth rate remains the same and the stock's P/E is unchanged, the rate of return will be twelve percent per year (two-percent yield plus ten-percent earnings growth).
4. You must be convinced that this twelve-percent return compensates you for the risk either that FPL growth slows down or that the stock's P/E drops over the years.

The interesting thing is, however, that the P/E actually can drop rather sharply and you can still have a fine investment, provided the earnings growth continues over a long enough period. As long as Florida Power and Light, for example, grows at a ten-percent rate over, say, ten years, the P/E can drop from twenty to sixteen or even lower and it can be termed an effective use of capital. A decline in P/E from twenty to sixteen, along with a ten-percent compounded earnings growth (and a two-percent dividend payout), will still allow the stock to show a ten-percent average rate of return, and this still compares favorably with a fixed-income investment such as a bond.

The slower-growth utilities can also experience a reduced P/E and come out well ahead as investments. A five-percent growth company over ten years can see its P/E drop from fifteen to less than twelve and (including, of course, the current yield of four percent) realize a six-percent return. As a matter of fact, the P/E can drop from fifteen to as low as nine and the average rate of return over ten years will still equal four and one-half percent.

All in all, I believe one can point to an average rate of return of at least eight percent from electric-utility stocks over a long period. With this in mind, I believe we can make two important conclusions, as follows:

1. For a portfolio which has time to wait, I would prefer large holdings of electric-utility stocks rather than huge proportions of bonds and other fixed-income securities.
2. Since results from electric utilities are among the most predictable, I would expect to achieve higher than the eight-percent average rate of return from other stocks with a less-predictable future. In other words, because of the uncertainties, other stocks should sell at a *lower* P/E than the electric utility with the same anticipated growth rate.

Obviously there are many non-utility companies which have shown superior consistency in earnings growth to that of the utilities. As we will see in the next chapter, it is this all-important element of *certainty of earnings growth* which is the key to the "proper" P/E to pay for a stock.

Before we explore this certainty element further, however, let me complete the discussion of *the importance of earnings growth*. I stated at the outset in this chapter that IBM could prove a decent investment even if we visualized a halving of its P/E in the future. This is only true if IBM's profits continue to advance at a compounded fifteen-percent rate. This combination of fifteen-percent growth and a cutting in half of the P/E over ten years still gives an overall investment return of eight percent (plus dividend returns) to IBM stockholders today. To further illustrate the importance of earnings growth, we could, in our search for an eight-percent return, afford only a one-third reduction in the P/E if IBM's growth averaged twelve and one-half percent per year; and if the company's growth rate were "only" ten percent per year, we could not stand more than a one-quarter reduction in the P/E and come out with an average eight-percent annual return on our dollars.

Thus, while the study of investments is all tied in with mathematics, the most important considerations will come from our *judgment of what the future holds.* While the following pages will take us further in improving our judgment, I felt an understanding of the mathematics absolutely essential. At any rate, Profit-Aid 6 has covered what constitutes the heart of all investment decisions: the annual rate of return on dollars risked. You have seen how professional advisors think—and this should give you the proper insight and a new perspective for the future use of your dollars.

Note: In reading the above, do not conclude that returns of 4½ to 8 percent per year are considered adequate or wholly satisfactory. They certainly are not! A growth investor should hardly be satisfied with less than ten-to-twenty-percent per annum. As a matter of fact, the real capital-gain-oriented investor should never buy a stock unless he can envision a return of well above such percentages. The illustrations above, however, do prove a point, and they set up a thinking process and an operating procedure which should be followed by security buyers regardless of objectives.

Chapter Five

The Importance of Being Certain

In the last chapter I discussed the importance to the investor of buying into a company which is going to grow in the future. Since history is a great teacher, security analysts look at a company's past with the thought that it might well be a key to its future. The trouble is, of course, that too many times a company's recent history may be completely misleading. Perhaps the company in question experienced excellent results over the last five years, since 1962, but then the record before 1962 might have been poor and therefore this "excellent growth" may exist only because your base year (1962 in this case) was a depressed year. Or perhaps the company's profit growth in recent years has been at the expense of the future (i.e., a land company selling off much of its properties and showing large and expanding net income—which, of course, will drop off sharply as the supply of land is used up). Or perhaps the company in question has benefited of late from some sort of fad, which will eventually taper down or even cease to exist.

Obviously, your assessment of a company is going to depend on what you visualize for its future. This is where clear, objective thinking is going to pay off. Anyone can look at a corporation's past record and extend it mathematically, but the person who foresees changes and who anticipates the future correctly is the one who is going to be successful in the stock market.

As a foundation, therefore, let me give you what I consider the correct approach to assessing the future of a company, through Profit-Aid 7. Briefly, this approach involves a magnifying-glass look at *the industry* in which a company is engaged—with stress on answering the following questions:

Is the industry still growing, or has it already reached maturity?

Do labor costs constitute a major hurdle for the industry to overcome?

Does the industry enjoy a firm price structure, or is it instead one which is constantly engaged in pricing battles?

Is it a field which is fairly immune to new competition?

Is it an industry which is extremely sensitive to the inevitable business cycles, or is it "recession-resistant"?

Once convinced that the industry in question passes these tests, the magnifying glass is then placed on the individual company you are considering—with the following important questions:

Does the company possess top management?

Does the company prepare correctly for the future with good research and development?

Is it diversified enough that one new "mousetrap" from a competitor will not endanger its position seriously?

Does the company have new products with good promise?

Is the corporation somehow protected in its operations by patents, technological know-how, etc.?

Has it been able to control costs correctly?

Following these logical steps leads you to a conclusion about the overall prospects for the outfit you are considering.

Then it is a matter of determining, as closely as possible, what kind of average growth rate you might expect in the next few years for the company—and then paying a P/E multiple which corresponds to such expected growth rate.

Now we come to the reason for this chapter, which is to emphasize *the importance of being certain about the future prospects for the company you are analyzing.* Needless to say, you should be willing to pay a premium for a company whose growth rate looks quite certain, as opposed to one which breathes of uncertainty. While the element of uncertainty will have come out in the industry-company approach I have dictated, I consider it essential to place extra stress here. For example, I would warn people today of the dangers existent in the multitude of small electronics companies which are (at the time of this writing) the "darlings" of the market. While there are many reasons for my skepticism, perhaps the main consideration involves the lack of certainty of success (products in the electronics field are bound to be subject to great obsolescence) for the vast majority of organizations engaged in this field. This is just one of many, many examples of uncertainty. Any business, for example, which is subject to changes in *style* should give you cause for concern. Referring to 1961, I found the public's enthusiasm for "cloak-and-suit" companies completely ridiculous. No matter what the recent record might show for a manufacturer of dresses, suits, coats, I would have a hard time building much enthusiasm for it. Why? Because a sudden change in style can erase profits in no time. And there is really no way to guard against such a change. The public is fickle about certain things, especially· clothes. When the fashion plates of the country suddenly turn sour on a particular style, the previous vogue becomes as popular as yesterday's newspaper. The manufacturers who have goods on their shelves now possess stale items which, almost regardless of price, have no market; inventory losses can wipe out profits rapidly, and what looked like a sound and healthy business suddenly reveals itself for what it truly is—a highly speculative enterprise, extremely sensitive to style changes.

Another example of relative uncertainty involves the aircraft manufacturers. While this group has had numerous vogue periods, conditions can change drastically in the defense-armament field. Of course, the most drastic change would be a discontinuation of the cold war—wherein aircraft-missile manufacturers would see their market vastly reduced in size. Admittedly, all-out peace appears rather remote, but even with the cold war the industry is fraught with shifts in demand. For one thing, one never knows who will be awarded what big contract from the government. Secondly, contracts are cancelable by the government (ask anyone who owned North American Aviation in 1957: out of a clear sky the company's Navajo missile contract was terminated, and the fortunes of North American were severely affected).

What I am leading to in this discussion is merely an extension of two of life's most practical axioms: first, about not being penny-wise and pound-foolish, and, second, about getting what you pay for in most things. So now we come to Profit-Aid 8—the following advice: *Give heavy weight to that industry or that stock which has a strong element of certainty to it; and realize that, most often, you will be better off paying some premium (i.e., a slightly higher P/E) for this as opposed to something which is somewhat cheaper but which has great uncertainties surrounding its future.*

While some investors feel that the best protection against downside risk is to pay the lowest possible P/E for a stock, those who have seen what a deterioration in earning power can do to a stock—regardless of its P/E at the beginning—know how foolish this reasoning is. Utilizing real-life illustrations again, I recall arguing vociferously in favor of people buying a quality company such as Hewlett-Packard for "certainty" representation in the electronics business—and emphasizing my willingness to pay a premium P/E for this company, as opposed to many, many others which lacked the certainty but which were available at lower multiples. Needless to say, there are countless examples similar to this, and the vast, vast majority of instances reveals what the Hewlett-Packard case did: that the best protection is to buy stock in the company with a certain growth future and that it is better to "pay up" some to get it rather than to downgrade and buy something which is fraught with uncertainties.

As an extension of this thinking, I am sure it will be useful for you to consider some of the most certain areas within our economy for growth.

As I see it, these areas include:

1. More air travel and air-cargo transportation.
2. More nuclear-energy utilization by the utilities.
3. More use of electricity.
4. Automation of all forms.
5. Burgeoning demands for mass rapid transit.
6. Increasing use of tunneling, excavation, and drilling— to place facilities of all sorts underground.
7. Greater demands for security and protection of resources, facilities, etc.
8. More dollars spent by consumers on:
    a. Leisure-time activities
    b. Convenience foods
    c. Products for personal health, sanitation, and adornment.

Naturally, an attempt to key investments to these certainties gives us that much better chance for success over the years. Thus, the value of the Profit-Aids provided in this chapter; both the philosophical and practical aspects have been covered for you!

Chapter Six

Reassessing a Company's Potential Earning Power

Stockholders and students of the market are continuously asking whether they should set a price goal for their stock purchases right from the beginning and then objectively stick to this goal and sell when it is reached. Obviously, the long-term, patient investor is *not* going to invest this way (he is looking for large, long-range gains and is content to "sit" on his good stocks). As you know, however, every smart investor should supervise his holdings periodically, with the thought of weeding out issues which have become overpriced. And the person who closes his eyes to price levels is simply not doing his job.

While, as mentioned earlier, I am opposed to large buying and selling activity in the stock market, I must reemphasize the importance of proper portfolio supervision—which brings me to the point in mind and to Profit-Aid 9, which is: *Reassess your stocks continuously and, when doing so, remember how time and circumstances may be changing the figures you are using.*

As they say, "Tempus does fugit" in life, and you will find

time fleeting by with your stocks, too; whereas one minute you are assessing 1967's potential earnings for XYZ Company, you will find it isn't long before 1967 is ancient history and that you are (or should be) already looking at 1968. Therefore, you cannot set a price goal on XYZ stock dogmatically, *without putting a time limit on this goal*. You might, however, use the following type of reasoning:

XYZ's past record and future potential make the stock deserve a price-earnings ratio of twenty. Last year the company earned $1.50 per share and this year the very maximum that can be expected is $2.00 per share. If the stock sells at twenty times the $2.00 earnings, then we might expect a $40 market price for XYZ stock. If the stock goes well above this figure *early in the year,* say, to $50 per share, investors are getting way ahead of themselves, and perhaps we should take advantage of this apparently inflated rise and sell XYZ at $50. But remember the time element! This $50 price looks juicy to us based on our assumption of approximately $2.00-per-share earnings for the year. But if this year is almost over, then the market is no doubt already looking to next year's possible performance by XYZ, and this may produce net income far greater than $2.00 per share. Or perhaps you can foresee next year's earnings being *lower,* in which case a price of only $35 or $30 will look high enough to sell XYZ stock.

Thus, it is a matter of constantly reassessing your company's outlook—quarter by quarter, year by year, all with an objective eye for determining what sensible investors should be paying for the stock.

Whatever you do, do not lose sight of both the foresight indicated as so essential in Chapter 1 and the understanding of how sophisticated investors are more interested in the future than in temporary interruptions. In short, the Big Picture look is far more important than relatively minor interim problems.

A fine example of this philosophy can be found in the market-price performance of Caterpillar Tractor stock throughout 1966 and to mid-1967. Despite a downward progression of earnings from a peak of $2.80 per share in 1965 to $2.65 in 1966 and to an estimated $2.00–$2.25 for 1967, "Cat" stock met consistent support in the $36–$39 price level, even during a generally weak market period in 1966. In addition, the stock traded in large volume in the mid-$40 area in 1967 —something which might have amazed the person who was not trained to think as I hope to get you thinking. After all, the latter price was at least twenty times projected results for 1967—certainly a hefty multiple for a company with cyclical tendencies (to be discussed in chapters 7 and 19).

The explanation for this buying interest in Caterpillar is really twofold, namely:

1. Stocks (and general markets) always take on a higher-than-normal P/E while earnings are depressed. Such a multiple is another way of saying that they (the earnings) are at or near bottom and that they will improve significantly later on.
2. The future Big Picture look may appear quite sensational, and sophisticated investors are more interested in this than in temporary jiggles.

In the case of Caterpillar, the 1968 outlook was hardly for anything dynamic—what with $2.40–2.70-per-share profits about all that could be expected. And 1969 probably promises no more than $2.80–3.00, so these 1967 prices were a high-enough fifteen times such two-years-hence estimates. Ah, but what then? Is there a possible explosion in potential earning power after 1969?

The purpose of this book is not to recommend individual securities, so we hope the readers will accept this as an illustration only (much can change between now and publication date and/or your reading date). I have seen some well-documented research, however, which projects Caterpillar's 1970 earnings in the $4.10–4.70 range, and it is an extension of these figures and the kind of thinking advanced in the previous few chapters which should prove as a fine example of what price to pay for a stock, the importance of being certain, and the need for consistent reassessment of any security.

Let us start with the element of certainty, which we will summarize by stating that Caterpillar is the peer in an industry which should grow sharply (albeit not evenly) due to domestic and world demands for equipment to build roads, dams, and other public-type construction projects. (Actually, Caterpillar's main problem in the 1966–1967 period was lack of capacity to handle demands and related expenses from building up such capacity.)

As to what price to pay, let's go through the kind of procedure advanced in our Zenith example in Chapter 2. Caterpillar stock has always commanded a premium in the market, and, considering its thirteen-percent annual compounded growth rate from a base of 1946–1950 to 1966, this was apparently deserved. More important, the management image and the apparently assured growth commencing in 1968 should support a decent P/E. Being fairly conservative, let us assume an approximate fifteen-times multiple for the stock. Relating this fifteen P/E to earnings of, say, $4.40 in 1970 gives a potential price of $66 at that time, or about sixty-five percent higher than the averaged $40 market price of 1967.

This in itself sounds intriguing enough, but let's relate it to other investments on an annual-rate-of-return basis (as in Chapter 4). An advance of sixty-five percent over a three-year span amounts to 18-percent annual compound growth. By adding Caterpillar's current dividend return (yield) of 2½ percent, the 1967 investor is looking at a possible 20+ percent annual increment from the stock. By relating this return to bond yields of 5½–6½ percent and to a variety of other equity and nonequity choices available, it becomes apparent how and why Caterpillar stock received the support it did during a down period. Apparently portfolio managers felt that potential rewards were sufficient to take the risk that the future might not develop as hoped for. In addition, the projected P/E of fifteen might prove to be low (Caterpillar has frequently enjoyed higher multiples in the past), and an assumption of just an eighteen P/E raises the annual-compound-growth figure from 20 to about 26 percent.

Conclusions

I am sure that no one has ever been advised to emulate the wretched Fagin from Dickens' *Oliver Twist*. And certainly I am not going to break this precedent. But the wonderful musical adaptation of this story—*Oliver!*—gives us one stock-market-lesson reminder. Toward the close of this production, Fagin sings "Reviewing the Situation," which of course is what all investors should do on a periodic basis. In doing so, be just as cold and ruthless as Fagin. Just as Fagin's life and prospects changed in *Oliver!*, you may find your stocks in an altered position and you may want to react accordingly. Some may look more attractive than ever, some may look discouraging—*but look at them and understand the wisdom of Big Picture reassessment as illustrated.*

Chapter Seven

How to Uncover
Cyclical-Growth Stocks

By the time you have completed this book I hope you, too, will become an advocate of buying stocks which have a growth pattern. As I will point out again and again, you can count on a company's growth in earnings to produce appreciation in the market price of its stock. This is because a growth in earnings leads (usually) to a growth in dividends; these two elements obviously lead to a growth in investor confidence; and the combination of these factors generally leads to considerable growth in market price.

Any person who recognizes the wisdom of this philosophy will in turn be negative on the cyclical companies. Why be burdened with the worries created by the ups and inevitable downs which cyclical companies experience either in sympathy with the general economy or with fluctuating demand for their own products? Why not instead buy companies which are exempt from these cyclical fluctuations and which have a strong enough inherent growth factor to withstand general economic declines? In other words, why buy trouble when you can avoid it?

The number of companies in existence which are completely resistant to recessions, however, is somewhat limited. There are countless very fine companies which experience minor interruptions in their growth patterns from time to time. In other words, the analysis of stocks is like life in general in that *the extremes are the exception; most people and things are "middle ground."* To look at a business enterprise which has deviated somewhat and experienced a few interruptions in its earnings pattern over a number of years and say unequivocally that it is therefore *not* a growth company is like saying that mistakes, or even growing-up periods, are not permitted in life. As mentioned, not all growth companies show increases in profits every year. Thus it is extremely important to distinguish between the inherent-growth company which is merely experiencing one of its very occasional cyclical downturns and the out-and-out cyclical company which we prefer to avoid. The major differences between these two are:

1. The growth company's products will have expanding markets, whereas the nongrowth outfit will be in a business which is pretty much at maturity.
2. The growth company's earnings decline will come less often than the typical cyclical entity which boasts little or no inherent growth.
3. The nongrowth company's business will be so sensitive to the business cycle that an overall business decline will lead to a drastic reduction in sales and profits, whereas the growth company's results will not be as severely affected.

In other words, as in any analysis, the key factors will lie in our appraisal of the industry in which the company is engaged; the company's position within this industry; the company's past performance and its chances for improving on this performance in the future.

Let's talk about this analysis of past performance a little further, because it is such an obvious clue to a cyclical company. Fortunately, past performances are public information in the stock market, and it is easy to spot a true cyclical company merely by glancing at its record and seeing the erratic behavior of profits in the past. But what about this in-between "cyclical-growth" company I have mentioned? Is there some way we can distinguish it from the cyclical enterprise? I believe there is a way to do this, and this is the main reason for this chapter.

Two Clues to Cyclical-Growth Stocks

How can we look at a company which experiences occasional declines in net income and determine that it is still on the way to better things? To aid you in finding this all-important answer, I have separated two important clues, which constitute Profit-Aid 10:

1. *Determine whether the company has earned more money in the latest "bad year" than in the previous bad year and in each one before that.*
2. *Instead of looking at the company's record year-by-year, take an average of a few years at a time and see what the trend is.*

Let's take a look at what was once a cyclical-growth company and see how this Profit-Aid gives us a far better insight into the company and its stock. To my way of thinking, we have a fine example in the Cummins Engine Company—a stock which was, at one time, a wonderful investment for its owners. Cummins' record for the eleven years from 1953–1963 was as shown on page 55.

You can see from this that Cummins' record was *not* one of consistent year-to-year growth such as we find in IBM, Bristol-Myers, Texas Utilities, etc. Sales grew from 1953 to 1957, but 1958 saw a minor decline; then 1959 showed a dramatic increase, but both 1960 and 1961 were down again, and then 1962–1963 came along with a sharp increase. As to Net Income Per Share, 1953 to 1956 were fantastic, but were fol-

Year	Net Sales (millions)	Net Income (millions)	Per Share Net Income
1963	$194.3	$13.51	$2.73
1962	167.3	10.62	2.15
1961	129.3	6.32	1.28
1960	135.8	6.03	1.23
1959	147.0	8.23	1.68
1958	108.8	3.90	.80
1957	111.2	5.10	1.06
1956	105.8	5.70	1.19
1955	81.0	4.52	.94
1954	59.2	2.88	.59
1953	56.0	1.62	.33

lowed by two years of sharp decreases; then 1959 more than doubled over 1958, only to see 1960 drop off substantially; 1961 was only slightly better than 1960, and then 1962 and 1963 produced spectacular results again.

Some people might not have rested easily with Cummins, despite the fact that both sales and earnings had done exceedingly well over this span. In this case, however, the base year, 1953, was a recession year in the United States and thus all comparisons with this year look excellent. Put yourself in the position of the investor considering Cummins stock in 1961, however. Chances are this prospective buyer would look back only five years, not ten, and this 1956–1960 period is certainly nothing to shout about. To ease this problem of worrying about which year to start with and which year we might have been considering the purchase of Cummins, I suggest we now look at the two Profit-Aid clues I have suggested using.

The first involves a comparison of bad years for the company involved. In the case of Cummins, sales and earnings have been directly sensitive to the business cycle in this country. Since World War II, we have experienced four recessions: 1949, 1953–1954, 1957–1958, and 1960–1961. Let's see how Cummins has fared in each of these recession periods:

Recession Year or Years	Cummins Earnings at That Time
1949	$0.21-per-share
1953–1954	0.47-per-share average
1957–1958	0.93-per-share average
1960–1961	1.25-per-share average

Cummins has obviously passed the first of our two tests: the company has earned more money (and by a substantial amount) in each successive trough. It doesn't take much logic to assume from this that Cummins had definite inherent growth which was making it more and more profitable over the years.

Now to our second test, which amounts to an averaging of the company's earnings instead of looking at each year by itself. Perhaps the most effective approach here is to construct a three-year moving average. This is very easily done, since all you have to do is take this year's results and add those of the last two years and divide by three. In our Cummins example, here is how the reported year-by-year profits are changed by constructing a three-year moving average:

Year	Earnings per Share as Reported	Three-Year Moving Average
1963	$2.73	$2.05
1962	2.15	1.56
1961	1.28	1.40
1960	1.23	1.24
1959	1.68	1.19
1958	.80	1.02
1957	1.06	1.06
1956	1.19	.91
1955	.94	.63
1954	.59	.44*
1953	.33	.48*

* Based on earnings per share not shown here: $.54 per share in 1952 and $.94 in 1951.

First of all, let me say that the three-year moving average is not a magic trick or hocus-pocus to alter basic figures. It is, of course, based on the reported figures, and all it really does is to even out the good and bad years. The important thing is its trend and, in the case of Cummins, you can see that this trend was sharply upward. Naturally, you have to have confidence in the future of Cummins and its business, but this average takes some of the emotion out of the statistics and it gives you a better picture of the company's real progress on a long-term basis. Looking at Cummins this way certainly restores your confidence and enables you to survey the company for what it was: a company which had been affected by the business cycle, but a growth company nonetheless.*

Based on our two tests, Cummins qualified as a cyclical-growth vehicle. The shortsighted investor might never have touched Cummins stock, or he might have bought it but subsequently might have panicked during one of the company's downturns. In either case, he would have been sorry, as the following history of the stock's market price over this eleven-year period indicates:

Year	Price Range of Common Stock†
1963	59⅝–46
1962	54⅜–32¾
1961	50¼–29¾
1960	30½–20⅛
1959	32⅝–21¾
1958	21½–11¼
1957	19 –11¾
1956	16½– 9⅜
1955	10½– 5¾
1954	5¼– 4¼
1953	5⅛– 3½

† Adjusted for stock dividends through 1963.

* Subsequent developments within Cummins' industry have probably made this thesis inaccurate; by 1968, there were serious doubts about the company's cyclical-growth position. Still, the illustration is valid for the period shown and through 1966, too.

I have already referred to a fine example of another cyclical-growth company, i.e., Caterpillar Tractor. So that you can see our method repeated, I have broken down the company's post-World War II record, constructed a three-year moving average, and shown the earnings achieved during each of the four recession periods.

Year	Reported Earnings per Share	Three-Year Moving Average	Recession Periods
1966	$2.64	$2.57	
1965	2.80	2.16	
1964	2.26	1.60	
1963	1.42	1.18	
1962	1.12	.97	
1961	1.01	.87 ⎫	$.89
1960	.77	.73 ⎭	
1959	.84	.71	
1958	.58	.77 ⎫	.65
1957	.72	.81 ⎭	
1956	1.02	.74	
1955	.70	.53	
1954	.50	.45 ⎫	.45
1953	.40	.38 ⎭	
1952	.44	.44	
1951	.30	.40	
1950	.57	.42	
1949	.34	.33*	.34
1948	.36	.25*	

* Not shown: 1947: $.28; 1946: $.12.

In conclusion, we know how important it is to be far-sighted instead of shortsighted. This is especially true when it comes to investments. In essence, I think all of the above has added to your foresight; and the Profit-Aid has given you objectivity and an unusual approach to the determination of what constitutes a typical cyclical company (in which we do not want to invest on a long-term basis) and what constitutes a cyclical-growth company—which can produce excellent investment results over the years.

Chapter Eight

"Going in the Back Door," or a Way to "Play" Mergers and Improving Situations with a Minimum of Risk

From time to time over an investor's life, the story or rumor of a potential merger or sale of a company will present itself. By the time the rumor has sifted down to the public it is not "inside information" any longer. Those who heard it first no doubt purchased stock of the company in discussion and thus there has probably been some advance in the price of the stock by the time the average investor gets his information. In other words, merger rumors—when "played" in the market —entail considerable risks for the following reasons:

1. The stock in question has probably had a rise already— a rise usually well above what the stock would sell for without the company merging or selling out.
2. The average investor will be among the last to know if merger negotiations fall through, or he will discover he has been wrong "after the horse is out of the barn door" —when the stock is already way down in price.

While this discussion is anything but encouraging, there's no denying that a lot of money has been made speculating on mergers and/or sellouts. I simply want to point out the risks involved and emphasize that this kind of buying is not "investing"; it is speculating and is therefore not suitable for most people.

There is, however, a way to "play" mergers, which is completely logical, which entails little risk, and yet which is usually considered only by the most astute and sophisticated investor and which is seldom thought of by the nonprofessional (and, as a matter of fact, is overlooked by most professionals, too). Profit-Aid 11, therefore, entails the following advice: *Consider the purchase of the fixed-income securities of the company to be merged rather than buying the company's common stock.*

People always think of how the common stock will benefit in the event of a merger or sellout, but they fail to consider the possible benefits to the company's preferred stock and/or bonds. Consider, for example, the theoretical case of the Bucket-o-Bolts Automotive Company. Bucket-o-Bolts has only a fair financial position and, because of this, its preferred stock and bonds outstanding fail to command a strong investment rating and thus sell pretty low in price in the market. But if Bucket-o-Bolts becomes a part of General Motors, the former's fixed-income obligations—that is, the Bucket-o-Bolts bonds and preferred stocks—suddenly take on real stature; the strong financial backing of GM now provides complete confidence in these securities by investors and the bonds and preferred stocks in turn sell at much higher prices than before.

In many cases, there might actually be *more* money made in a merger through purchase of the merging company's bonds and/or preferred stock than through purchase of the common stock—even though the risk factor in the former might be far less than in buying the common. Take, for example, the case of Philco Corporation before it was merged into Ford Motor Company in the latter part of 1961. Philco, formerly a very successful appliance manufacturer, had run into operating difficulties in 1961 and had begun piling up sizable losses. These losses naturally shook investor confidence in all

Philco securities—which came down in price. Whereas a year earlier Philco common stock was selling in the $30 range and its $3.75 (this is the annual dividend rate) preferred stock was selling around $70, August 21, 1961, found Philco common at $21 and the preferred at $63. It was at that time that rumors of a Ford-Philco merger began to circulate—followed by an announcement of the proposed merger. Within a few months, these Philco securities rose as follows:

| | COMMON STOCK | | PREFERRED STOCK | |
	Price	*Rise since* *August 21*	Price	*Rise since* *August 21*
September 8	23⅛	10%	74	17%
September 22	22⅝	8%	93	48%
November 10	23½	12%	96¼	53%

By the time the merger was consummated (December 11), the common was at 25¼, while the preferred was at 100. Thus, over the four-month span from August to December, the common advanced slightly over twenty percent—and the preferred increased over fifty-eight percent! An investor would have made almost triple profits from the preferred compared with the common. And the interesting fact is that the preferred buyer probably took far *less* risk at the outset than the buyer of the common.

Recovery Situations
The very same reasoning about maximizing profits with a minimum of risk in corporate mergers with Profit-Aid 11 can be utilized successfully when investing in previously sick companies which are making a comeback. These comeback companies (called "recovery situations" in the investment world) offer intriguing possibilities. Dynamic appreciation possibilities generally exist in previously successful companies which are restored to meaningful profitability again or in companies which are suddenly coming into their own for the first time. Naturally you will benefit in such a turnabout from buying the company's common stock, but you might do just

as well or even better—and generally with less risk—from buying its preferred stock or bonds.

Consider the J. I. Case Company as it existed in 1962–1963. Case has long been one of the nation's largest manufacturers of farm machinery and implements. But size alone is no investment criterion. Despite sales exceeding $100 million, Case incurred large losses in both 1960 and 1961. Because of this bleak picture, all of Case's publicly held securities came down sharply in price. Case common, which was over $20 per share in 1960 and 1961, dropped into the $5–$10 range in 1962; the Case $7.00 preferred, which was formerly in the $100–$120-per-share area, slumped about in half as its dividend was omitted; and the company's $0.455 preferred, which also passed its dividend payment, fell from $5–7 per share to about $3.00. All in all, the Case picture was not at all a pretty one, and all the company's securities were affected.

During 1962, management went to work to clean up the mess which existed. By the second quarter of that year, Case was beginning to show improvement; as a matter of fact, the company broke even in this period, compared to a loss incurred in the second quarter of 1961. This was a clue at least to a partial recovery, as was the third quarter—in which Case showed a small profit (compared to a good-sized loss in the previous year). Despite this improvement and the enhanced prospects for the fourth quarter (which ended October 31), Case stocks remained depressed. As late as December 17, its stocks were selling at the following prices on the New York Stock Exchange:

Case common stock	$ 6
Case $7.00 preferred, which now carried arrears* of $13.00 per share	$54
Case $0.455 preferred, which now carried arrears* of $0.91 per share	$ 2⅝

* Arrears are unpaid dividends which are owed to the preferred stockholders and which must be paid in full before the common stockholders can get any dividends at all.

If you believed in the recovery prospects of Case, you could have bought any of these three securities. Profit-Aid 11 would have reminded you that: *Recovery in the company* (*and the common stock*) *could hardly have taken place without the money owed to the preferred stockholders* (*the arrears—as shown above*) *being cleared up.* With this in mind, it is rather obvious that the two preferred issues held attraction. After all, the first preferred had $13.00 per share owing to it and promised to pay $7.00 per share annually in dividends if and when the company became profitable again— and yet it was selling at a figure of only $54.00 per share. And the second preferred, which had $0.91 per share due it and a possible $0.455 annual dividend, was selling for only $25⁄8.

Shortly after this December 17 date, Case reported its fourth-quarter results, which evidenced considerable improvement. All of a sudden, investors realized what was happening at Case—that the huge operating losses were at least temporarily halted, that the company had a chance of returning to profitability, that the preferred stocks suddenly held a remote chance of having their arrearages paid and returning to a regular dividend-paying basis again, and that the common stockholders had a chance for life again.

The market reacted accordingly. The two preferred issues discussed and the Case common stock suddenly traded in large volume on the Exchange and experienced the following performance in the ensuing weeks after the fourth-quarter announcement:

	Market Price on 12/17/62	Market Price on 1/2/63	Rise since 12/17/62	Market Price on 1/10/63	Rise since 12/17/62
Common	$ 6.00	$ 7.00	16%	$ 8.12	35%
$7.00 Preferred	54.00	67.00	24	76.50	41
$0.455 Preferred	2.62	3.37	28	3.87	47

As you can see, all three securities did well in these few weeks after the encouraging announcement, but the two preferred issues outperformed the common stock by a definite margin, despite the fact that they no doubt entailed less risk when originally purchased than did the common stock.

This is not to say that a bond or preferred stock in a company like Case does not carry risk with its purchase. If a company is forced into bankruptcy, chances are that no security will fare well. The bondholders might emerge with something worthwhile, but chances are very strong that the preferred stockholders will get little or nothing—nor, of course, will the common shareholders. In Case's example, a continuation of losses would have placed it in bankruptcy and the two preferreds would no doubt have fared no better than the common. Perhaps then you're wondering why I state that these two preferred issues entailed less risk than the common at the beginning. This is because a *temporary* improvement in Case's picture might have cleared the way for the payment of arrearages, and the fact that the preferreds would have to receive all of these unpaid dividends plus current dividend obligations before the common received so much as a dime gave the former a distinct advantage over the common. Thus, there was a better chance for success in the preferreds, which is another way of saying that they entailed less risk than the common.

Conclusions
I should point out that this method of "playing" mergers or recoveries through buying the fixed-income securities available is *not* the road to huge *long-term* profits. The biggest gains will no doubt come from owning the common stock of the merging company (in our example, Ford Motor) or of the recovering company (J. I. Case), and it is very seldom that holders of straight bonds or preferred stocks will end up with common stock. Thus, if you anticipate a merger and you like the prospects for long-term growth of the surviving, combined unit—you should plan on owning the common stock of this unit and should therefore be buying the common of the

company which is being bought out rather than its bonds or preferred stock; by the same token, if you prefer long-range equity ownership in a recovering company, you should consider purchasing its common outright.

On the other hand, Profit-Aid 11 gives you a minimum-risk-maximum-reward approach for near-term profits. I am certain you will see situations similar to our Philco and Case illustrations at some time in the future, and utilization of this Aid—the purchase of depressed fixed-income securities—may produce similar comparative results and may prove more intelligent than buying common stock.

Chapter Nine

Finding Companies Which Leave Investors Little Choice

One of the least sad tales of woe I have heard concerns the man who couldn't make up his mind which Cadillac to buy— the blue, red, or white one. He loudly complained, "Decisions, decisions, decisions. All day long, decisions." Farfetched? Not really. Because almost everyone, it seems, hates to make decisions.

Naturally this universal shortcoming in human nature pertains to the stock market, too. People refrain from buying and refrain from selling because of their reluctance to form conclusions and take action. It stands to reason, therefore, that if we can find an area in the market which gives people little choice—in which they have to fall in line—we have a better chance for success.

Profit-Aid 12 is presented with this thought in mind. It entails: finding stocks which have a better-than-average chance for success *because they constitute practically the only representative in their particular industry.*

Let's explore this. Assume now that you are especially attracted to a particular industry and that you have decided that you want to place some dollars into this area. If there are only a few individual companies within this group, your decision will be simplified. Let's say your choice is limited to Companies A, B, and C. No more! Provided that other people get the same idea and that just so many millions of dollars are going to be invested in the industry group, the amount will be far more heavily concentrated if the choice is only A, B, and C rather than if there are one or two *dozen* companies from which to choose. What this means, of course, is that A, B, or C should do far better for you than if the same amount of money were spread out among many different stocks.

Thus, if you like an industry it is better to have only a few top representatives because, if you are right in your appraisal of the prospects and eventually investors recognize this and commence buying, the money will pour into just a few issues and you will witness a greater proportionate rise. This supply-demand situation is just like a practical illustration of a large pitcher of water; if you pour the contents of the pitcher into twelve glasses, you will have a small amount in each glass; if, instead, you pour it into only three glasses, "the cup runneth over." In short, the market results from choosing an attractive industry with a limited number of participants are greatly magnified.

This is not to say that you cannot make money investing in industries which have many participants and many individual companies into which dollars can flow. After all, industries like oil and chemicals have countless publicly held companies from which to choose and yet a great deal of money has been made through their investment. But this does not refute the theory. What it means is that the group has to have enough qualities to attract many more dollars if most of the companies within the group are to be greatly successful marketwise. In other words, the fact that many participants exist must be looked upon as a negative—a weakness. As with any weakness, it behooves you to find enough strengths to compensate and overcome the disadvantages. Naturally, when there are enough strengths the existence of many companies should not bother you.

In a more positive vein, it can be exceptionally profitable to discover "limited industries" with just a few potential investments. Think, for example, of the success of Minnesota Mining and Manufacturing. A great deal of this company's success has been due to its extremely efficient management and its ability to earn more money year after year for its shareholders. But the stock's success can be attributed in part to the fact that the company stood for many years pretty much by itself in the tape field. There were many investors, both institutional and individual, who were simply attracted to the future of tape (magnetic, cellulose, etc.). They saw a future for tape products and they wanted a share in this growth. After assessing the field, most came to the simple conclusion that MMM was the place for such dollars of investment. For some time, MMM was practically the only company in the field, and thus all "tape dollars" flowed into its stock.

By the same token, Owens-Corning-Fiberglas enjoyed considerable stock-market success because the investor had almost no choice other than OCF. If you believed in the future of Fiberglas you had no further decision to make. It was not like investing in oil, in which you could choose from as many as four different Standard Oils, as well as Texaco, Phillips, Continental, Gulf, Shell, Pure, Union, Signal, and a host of others. This limited-choice, limited-decision situation was directly responsible for a good part of whatever success OCF enjoyed in the market. For example, despite a record of earnings decline from 1959 to 1962, OCF stock still commanded a price-earnings ratio of about twenty-five times (a high evaluation).

The dramatic rise in the bowling twins, AMF and Brunswick, was also partly due to the characteristic of limited choice.

Now—to make Profit-Aid 12 practical (and potentially profitable)—here is a list of some limited-choice areas in today's market. These include:

Controls, as dominated by Honeywell (with but a few other publicly held competitors).

Credit-rating, pretty much monopolized by Dun & Bradstreet.

Electrical equipment: GE and Westinghouse the prominent ones, along with Babcock & Wilcox and Combustion Engineering in the generating-equipment business.

Farm equipment: Most manufacturers are involved in other heavy machinery, too. Deere stands out as having little outside dilution; also, Caterpillar and Massey Ferguson.

Glass, with Corning leading the basic research and new-product development.

Photography, having Eastman and Polaroid as the prominent choices among only a handful (Bell & Howell, General Aniline).

Private aircraft, represented mainly by Beech, Cessna, and Piper.

Protection Services, including A.D.T., Burns, and Pinkerton's.

Tunneling machinery (for mass rapid transit, underground cabling, etc.), with Joy Manufacturing and Smith Industries.

Actually, I should point out that the number of companies alone is not the sole criterion in determining how much effect dollars pouring in will have. The consideration of *total market evaluation* is even more important than number of participants. Take the case of the automobile manufacturers. Leaving out American Motors for the moment, today's investor really has only the choice of the Big Three (Chrysler, Ford, and General Motors) if he has "automotive dollars" to invest. But does that mean that these individual stocks are slated to skyrocket upon the first blush of demand for the industry? Hardly so, simply because there are many millions of shares outstanding of the Big Three. What with GM's two hundred and eighty-six million shares, Ford's one hundred and fifteen million and Chrysler's forty-six million, you can see that there is no paucity of supply available. By multiplying the existing market prices by the aforementioned shares, you come up with the following market evaluation of the auto industry (as represented by the three):

	Shares Outstanding	Market Price	Total Evaluation
General Motors	285,679,000	$85	$24,283,000,000
Ford Motor	114,783,000	50	5,739,000,000
Chrysler	45,755,000	50	2,288,000,000
		Total	$32,310,000,000

Thus, the total market evaluation of these three amounts to the hefty sum of thirty-two billion dollars. This is another way of saying that it will take many dollars of demand to put a dent in the supply and drive the prices up exorbitantly. In comparison, let's look at the figures on the private aircraft builders:

	Shares Outstanding	Market Price	Total Evaluation
Beech	2,937,000	$50	$147,000,000
Cessna	3,359,000	49	165,000,000
Piper	1,628,000	55	89,000,000
		Total	$401,000,000

Needless to say, a tremendous disparity should exist between the market's appraisal of private aircraft vs. automobiles. The former account for only about four hundred and fifty million dollars each year in sales, whereas the latter represent approximately thirty-eight billion dollars annually in revenues. Still, the potential leverage in the tiny comparative capitalizations of Beech, Cessna, and Piper under the right psychological conditions must be obvious.

Because of all this, you have to expect to pay some kind of a premium (in the form of a higher P/E than might appear justified) when you buy into a limited-choice or limited-capitalization industry which is already recognized for its potentials by investors. And you certainly realize that your discovery of an industry group which might capture the imagination of the public and which has only a few companies from which to choose can be very explosive. Therefore, our industry list on page 70, while constituting no specific recommendation for purchase, at least alerts you to some "cup-runneth-over" areas of the market—with the obvious potentials.

Chapter Ten

Choosing a Guide to Determine
What to Expect from Your Stocks

From time immemorial investors have been puzzled and confused over the inability to determine just where their stocks
should be selling in the marketplace. Most of this difficulty
exists because the stock market in general is so very difficult
to assess on a day-to-day, week-to-week basis. Did I say difficult? I should have said "impossible." One of the truly frus-
trating things in life is the attempt to determine where the
general market will be in a short period of time. Over the
long term—over a period of a number of years—I think it is
safe to assume that the market (or I should really say the
"right" stocks) will eventually trend higher. Growth in earnings over a period of time should eventually counteract any
short-term negative psychology, and one should take the optimistic view that time is to your advantage.

But patting a person on the head and repeating the age-
old, slightly worn advice, "Patience, my boy, patience," can
be little consolation when your stocks are standing still or declining in value.

While I study many technical and fundamental items

73

which might have a bearing on the market, I have always felt that it is more important to stress the value of stocks *individually* rather than to concentrate on guessing (and it really is guessing) where the market in general might be next week or next month. Naturally this generalization has its exceptions; if, for example, the market looks like it is grossly overpriced and that it is on the brink of a sudden decline, these overall feelings would have a definite bearing on the retention or purchase of even the best stocks. But such extreme peaks occur very infrequently—they are very definitely the exception to the rule.

The reason that judgment of day-to-day market behavior is a matter of guesswork is that so many intangibles are involved. Whereas your success in holding an individual stock over a few years is going to depend mainly on tangible items such as industry results, company earnings and growth, dividends, etc., the assessment of near-term market behavior is going to be sensitive to many intangibles and nonpredictables, in addition to a variety of tangibles. Who knows, for example, what political, economic, international, or other developments are going to crop up and become the center of attention next week? And, more important, who knows how the public is going to react to same? These intangibles are far less predictable than the direction of earnings and dividends of companies such as American Telephone, General Foods, and others.

Despite this emphasis on selecting sound individual values as opposed to devoting a lot of time to day-to-day market behavior, there are some useful tools which will give you an idea of what to expect from your stocks on a shorter-term basis. One such tool, which is our Profit-Aid 13, is *to gauge the market against a few accepted blue-chip issues in which the investment community has a right to have complete confidence*. Take a stock such as IBM, for example. Historically, IBM has commanded a price-earnings multiple well above the market in general. Because of the company's consistent and rapid growth rate, as well as its commanding position in a glamorous industry, IBM's premium appears well justified.

The early part of 1963 serves as an illustration of using a stock like IBM as a gauge of what to expect. In March of that year, the general stock market, as measured by the Dow Jones Industrial Average, was selling for about twenty times the earnings expected for the full year (earnings for the combined stocks in the Dow Jones Average). At that time, IBM stock was selling for just over thirty times its anticipated 1963 per-share profits. While this difference of fifty percent (thirty times multiple for IBM *vs.* twenty times for the Average stocks) amounted to a healthy premium, a look at the past suggested that it was well below its "normal" relationship. In the 1958–1960 markets, for example, it was common to find IBM selling around forty times earnings, while the general market was trading in the seventeen-to-twenty-times area. Then, in the rampant bull market of 1961, this automation king ran up to sixty times earnings, while the Average stocks were selling for twenty-two to twenty-three times. The conclusion from this might be: provided that there had been no radical change in IBM's fundamental picture, it would be hard to conceive of the market advancing much further without this individual favorite leading the way. In other words, it was logical to assume that stocks with decidedly slower growth rates and with less certain futures would not advance much past twenty times earnings unless IBM had gone to multiples above thirty. Thus, IBM was a key stock which necessitated close watching, since it figured to serve as a good clue to the behavior of other stocks and the market in general.

The theory of using General Motors as a general market criterion follows the same principle. First of all, the auto business is so important to the whole economy and to so many other industries and companies. If weakness in GM stock emanates from anticipation of poor new-car sales in the near future, then many other industry groups should also feel a pinch—and their stocks can be expected to react accordingly.

A second reason for using GM as a market bellwether stems from the realization that it serves as a good indicator of investor confidence (or lack of confidence). Over the years, this corporate giant has served as a good barometer of investor psychology. Realizing that many stock buyers do not want to be bothered with complicated decisions in their purchases and instead theorize that "if things are good, GM is bound to benefit," a great many "confident" dollars just naturally flow into GM stock.

Naturally, as in the case of IBM, one has to judge whether fundamentals and prospects have changed for the company individually before utilizing the theory that it is a good judge of overall stock-market conditions.

Thus, while there is no one infallible formula, the assessment of a few secure and consistent stocks can give you fine insight into investor psychology—which in turn will help you determine what you might expect from other stocks on a near-term basis. Obviously, this method is no market forecaster, but it should aid your timing considerably. It should place other stocks in a good perspective and should provide you with a framework of reference by which you will be able to make more intelligent decisions in your buying and selling.

To supplement the theory behind Profit-Aid 13, I have compiled a list of what I consider key stocks or key industries —against which you will be able to base many decisions in the future. In so doing, I have separated the "models" according to their growth classification in the market. I have done this both because the market so often has crosscurrents running through it and because it is generally more reliable to judge stocks according to comparable issues. Thus, my comments on IBM were related to other fast-growth issues rather than to all stocks; and my remarks on GM were really more directed to comparable sensitive-to-the-economy stocks than to everything.

With this in mind, it makes more sense to judge timing against close counterparts, and I have constructed four categories for you to utilize, namely Rapid Growth, Above-Average Consistent Growth, Slow Growth, and Cyclical. In short, Profit-Aid 13 really becomes a specific Timing Guide, which entails your following this procedure:

1. When considering any stock for purchase, it should be simple enough for you to categorize it and place it against one of the four groups mentioned.

2. A check to see how the representative stocks in this category are selling in the market—compared with the various P/E multiples as shown in our Profit Guide— will tell you the "story" of investor confidence at that time.

3. Consider your intended purchase within this framework and go through the thinking process indicated in some of the prior chapters.

Now for the four categories and their representatives. In presenting these, I have shown the approximate multiples which might be expected in *their own* bull markets, static markets, and bear markets. Let me emphasize that you must consider *all* the representatives in the group (which eliminates the chance that one might be suffering some individual problems at the moment). Here we go:

APPROXIMATE P/E MULTIPLES "NORMAL" FOR THEIR OWN:

	BULL MKTS.	STATIC MKTS.	BEAR MKTS.
Fast Growth			
Bristol-Myers	40	30	25
Eastman Kodak	35	25+	22–23
Litton Industries	35	28	20
Minnesota Mining	35	28	20
IBM	40+	35	30
Above-Average Consistent Growth			
Borden	20	16	12
Dow Chemical	25	20	15
General Electric	25	20	17
Procter & Gamble	25	20	17
Sterling Drug	28	24	20
Texas Utilities	28	22	18

APPROXIMATE P/E MULTIPLES "NORMAL" FOR THEIR OWN:		
BULL MKTS.	STATIC MKTS.	BEAR MKTS.

Slow Growth

	BULL MKTS.	STATIC MKTS.	BEAR MKTS.
Del Monte Foods	16	14	12
First National City Bank (N.Y.)	16	14	12
Colgate-Palmolive	20	16	12
Standard Oil of Calif.	14	12½	10
Utility (Electric) Average	20	16	13

Cyclical

Anaconda	12	10	8
General Motors	15	13	11
International Harvester	12	10	8
Jones & Laughlin Steel	12	10	8
Railroad Average	12	10	8

Naturally, the above is no more than a guide, and I am, as mentioned, prone to buy a stock if it looks to possess a bright future and if it is not astronomical in price, rather than to be too price-conscious. This is only an extension of the thought about being penny-wise and pound-foolish (Chapter 5). On the other hand, we should always have some framework of reference as to where things stand at the moment, and reference to the above should be helpful to you for this purpose.

Chapter Eleven

Uncommon Profits
from Noncommon Stocks

A. HOW A PREFERRED STOCK CAN ACTUALLY BE
PREFERRED

Most security analysts and investment advisors and counselors agree that a preferred stock is a hybrid security in that it offers neither the extreme safety of a good bond nor the appreciation possibilities of a common stock. Indeed, the title "preferred" is a misnomer, because it is really not preferred (by many) at all.

While I agree with this reasoning, I hate to accept common beliefs as the gospel. As a matter of fact, it is especially wise when you are dealing with the stock market to question any and all common beliefs and unanimous opinions and to try instead to do some original thinking of your own. Actually, I hope this whole book is full of such original thinking—and this chapter attempts to parallel this philosophy.

I am not going to refute the fact that a bond of a company ranks ahead of its preferred stock in both the payment of annual income to its holders and in being first in line for distribution of assets in the event of the company's liquidation.

And obviously I am not going to argue the fact that a company's common stock offers far greater appreciation possibilities than its preferred stock. Nor am I even going to contend that preferred stocks generally are attractive at all. But I am going to argue that the person considering a fixed-income investment in a good company should *not* blindly buy its bond as against its preferred stock. In fact, as you will now see, I am going to argue strongly for buying *certain* preferred stocks *instead of bonds*.

The best tactician—whether it involves athletics, war, gambling, or what-have-you—places himself in the position of his opponent. In our case we have no opponent, but I want you to place yourself in the position of a corporation which needs money and is considering the sale of either bonds or preferred stock to fill this need. As you know, the corporation will be obligated to pay interest to its bondholders (if it decides to sell bonds) and to pay dividends to the preferred stockholders (if it chooses this method of financing). Despite the fact that these potential payments to the bondholders or preferred stockholders are fixed, the tax treatment of these payments *to the corporation* will differ dramatically. In short, *any interest paid to bondholders will be deductible in full before federal income taxes for the corporation, while any dividends on preferred stock will* not *be deductible at all*. Let's assume that the money we need will cost us $500,000 a year in either interest or preferred dividends. If we sell bonds, this $500,000 is fully deductible from net income and reduces our profits *before taxes* by this amount. Since the corporate-income-tax rate is about fifty percent, this deduction "saves" us the fifty percent we would have had to pay on the $500,000 if it were part of net income—and thus our company's tax bite is reduced by $250,000 (50 percent of $500,000 = $250,000).

If, instead of bonds, we decide to market preferred stock, we will have no such deduction. Thus, we will have to pay a fifty-percent tax on the full amount of net income and then distribute the $500,000 preferred dividend out of what is left. *The result is that our corporation—by using preferred stock*

*instead of bonds—is "out" the $250,000 in cash we would
have saved by using tax-deductible bond interest.*

I think the following table will illustrate this better. In this
example I have assumed that our corporation earned two million dollars before taxes, before allowing for the $500,000
figure. I have shown you specifically how the company will
fare under the bond issue and under that of a preferred
stock.

	A *If Company Raises Capital Through Issuance of Bonds*	B *If Company Raises Capital Through Issuance of Preferred Stock*
Our Net Income *Before* Taxes and Interest Charges Is	$2,000,000	$2,000,000
Less: Interest Expense on Bonds	500,000	None
Net Income Before Taxes	$1,500,000	$2,000,000
Less: Federal Income Taxes (50-percent rate)	750,000	1,000,000
Net Income After Taxes	$ 750,000	$1,000,000
Less: Dividends Paid on Preferred Stock	None	500,000
Cash Left out of Net Income for Common Stockholders	$ 750,000	$ 500,000

You can see that our company has $750,000 left for the
owners (common stockholders are the true owners of a
corporation) by using bonds to raise the needed capital, as
opposed to only $500,000 left by utilizing preferred stock.

Now to the reason for this explanation. I am not trying to
make corporate financiers out of you. My objective in this

book is to show you how to make money with your investments—not how to manage a business. But this discussion has a very practical significance which will lead us to an interesting, and I suggest profitable, conclusion.

It should be obvious from my illustration that a corporation will prefer the existence of bonds in its capital structure rather than preferred stock, wherever possible. Now, think of the countless preferred stocks that exist in this country today —and tell me your reaction. I know my reaction: *that certain companies may, over the years, come to the decision to substitute new bonds for existing preferred stock, so they can reduce their income-tax load and conserve cash.*

Many preferreds may not appear suitable for such substitution because the terms of their original issue stipulated that they would *not* be redeemable by the corporation; these preferreds are noncallable by the company and are a permanent fixture in its capitalization. The noncallable feature does not preclude its elimination, however. A corporation can make any offer it chooses to the stockholders. It cannot force redemption, but it can (and there have been many cases of this) make an offer attractive enough so that preferred holders will be happy to accept.

The majority of preferreds outstanding are redeemable and have a set call price at which the company can buy them back. Here is where we come to my thesis, which is our Profit-Aid 14, as follows: *Instead of buying bonds, buy (very select) preferred stocks selling well under their call price which look to have the potential for redemption—at prices well above current levels.*

What with money rates as high as they currently are, the market is filled with preferreds selling twenty to thirty dollars under their redemption values. If you can receive comparable income (and almost comparable safety) to a bond from these preferreds (and you can), then why shouldn't you avail yourself of this added capital-gain potential? I contend you should!

Remember that I said "certain preferreds," though. I do not recommend willy-nilly purchase of all preferred stocks just because they are selling at a sizable discount from their redemption price. I stated at the outset of this discussion that preferred stocks are not as stable, not as secure, as comparable bonds. As a matter of fact, if a company gets into financial difficulty, its bondholders will generally fare all right, whereas the claims of preferred stockholders are seldom settled to their satisfaction. Why, then, you might ask, do I say you should buy certain preferreds *in place of* buying bonds? You should buy them with the same purpose that you buy bonds (i.e., for safe income)—but with the knowledge that you are also buying a possible "kicker" which may line your pockets better. I am not suggesting that you buy these preferreds as you would common stocks—with chance for near-term profits (you may have to wait many years for your company to decide on redemption of its preferred) or for substantial long-term gains. Since you are buying these discount preferreds with the philosophy I suggest, you do not want to assume much risk and thus *I recommend only that you consider high-quality preferred issues.* As a matter of fact, the top-quality companies give you a better chance for success in this type of venture, because they boast strong financial positions and are thus better able to redeem their preferreds (they have more available cash to redeem them outright, and their financial strength better allows them to refinance with a bond issue, if they choose).

In your specific choices of preferreds you stand a better chance of redemption with a company which is not already heavily leveraged (laden with large amounts of bonds ahead of the preferred stock). A company without such complications has a clearer road to achieving redemption and you correspondingly have a better chance for success in your purchase. This thinking rules out securities of the public-utility companies, most of which have numerous fixed-income securities in existence and which are constantly raising new money for expansion (thereby issuing *new* securities, as opposed to redeeming old ones). As a matter of fact, the number of possible to-be-redeemed preferred stocks within the market is actually quite small; this complicates the problem of selection, although it certainly does not rule out the potential.

In conclusion, I have indicated throughout this book that successful investing involves a constant appraisal of *risk* vs. *rewards*. It never makes sense to take a sizable risk for but a small possible reward. By corollary, it makes excellent sense to invest where your risk is negligible and your possible rewards are *comparatively* large. It is because this latter circumstance exists that I suggest certain preferred issues to you. Just remember that this is anything but a get-rich-quick scheme. It should be approached only by the person who wants some fixed-income investments anyway—and simply chooses this channel because it at least offers a possible bonanza for him at some time in the future. I grant you that the potential gains are not large (perhaps fifteen to thirty percent), but the risks might be minimal. At any rate, we have now opened up a new facet of investing—and at least you can see that preferred stocks might sometimes really be preferred.

B. CONVERTIBLE SECURITIES—RISKS, REWARDS, AND A GUIDE FOR THEIR PURCHASE

Basic to this discussion is a knowledge of the ins and outs of *convertible* preferred stocks and convertible bonds. Briefly, the convertible feature takes these preferred stocks and bonds out of the category of strict fixed-income securities which have very limited chance for capital appreciation. When an investor buys a straight (nonconvertible) preferred or bond, he does so for its stable income and because it lacks much risk. In short, the buyer knows his annual income is quite secure but he also realizes that he is giving up large capital-gain potentials and a hedge against inflation. If the company issuing the preferred or bond adds a conversion feature to it, however, then an otherwise unexciting security has glamour to it. This is because the conversion feature gives the owner the right to exchange the bond or preferred for a designated number of common shares at the owner's choice over a given period of time.

Let's compare the investor's position when investing in the XYZ Company's bond when it is straight and when it has a conversion feature. In the first instance, you buy the bond strictly for the annual interest it will pay you, perhaps five percent; the bond will have a maturity date of perhaps twenty years hence, and thus you also know that you will receive your investment back intact at the end of that period. Because of the maturity date, your appreciation prospects are extremely limited, since the closer it gets to maturity the closer the bond will sell at its designated maturity price. (Who is going to pay much over $100 for a bond when it is going to mature in a year or two for $100?) The investor in this XYZ bond is interested in the company itself only in that he wants to be sure it has the money to pay the interest every year and the funds are on hand to pay him back at maturity. Other than that, the company's progress is of little concern, since the bondholder is only a creditor of the company and is *not* an owner. XYZ might become the finest growth company in the country over the years and the XYZ bondholder will realize no appreciation prospects from this great progress.

On the other hand, if the XYZ bond gives its owner the right to exchange the bond for a certain number of common shares, then the company's progress is of great importance. Assume, for example, that XYZ common stock is now selling at $8.50 per share; assume also that the new XYZ convertible bond due in 1987 gives its owners the right to exchange each $100 bond * for ten shares of common stock anytime

---

* Actually, most bonds are *traded* in $1,000 denominations, not $100. Their market prices are quoted, however, in $100 terms (for convenience), and I have utilized the $100 example because it is simpler and because it is standard procedure. If you place an order for bonds, you are normally committing yourself to $1,000 denominations, even though they are quoted in $100's. Thus, if you order "five bonds," you are usually buying $5,000, not $500. I think it best to clarify this, lest someday you order more than you desire.

over the bond's life. Naturally, the bondholder is not going to exchange the $100 bond into ten shares of common when the common is selling for only $8.50. (Why exchange a security worth $100 for $85 worth of common?) But if XYZ common rises to $12, then the ten-share conversion privilege gives the bond a minimum value of $120 (10 × $12 = $120). And if XYZ common rises to $40, then the bond contains a value of $400 (10 × $40 = $400). Thus, the conversion feature gives the bond similar potentials to its common stock. At the same time, the bondholder knows his income is safer than if he were receiving dividends on common stock (bond interest has to be paid in full before any dividends are paid on the common), and thus many investors conclude that there is really little or no risk in buying convertible securities; they contend that this is one case where you can have your cake and eat it, too.

Actually, there are many convertible issues where you really do have little or no downside risk and still possess capital-gain potentials. This would occur when you buy the bond of a top-flight company (where you have no worry about the safety of interest payments) at such a price that it (the bond) would sell even if it had no conversion privilege whatsoever. Then, even if the convertible aspect were never of any benefit to you—that is, even if the common stock never rose enough to make the bond worth more—you would know that the bond would sell at about the same price just for its income benefits. Of course, you would never have such a guarantee when buying the bond of a lesser-quality company, in which the interest and the chance for repayment of principal at maturity would hold uncertainties. I have heard too many people say something like the following: "How can I possibly lose money buying the Hula Hoop Mfg. Co. bond when it is paying six percent?" You'd be surprised! Small companies usually lack real security, and the slightest hint of financial weakness can cause a drastic erosion in the price of both their stocks *and* bonds. This Hula Hoop six-percent bond which looked riskless at $100 can drop to $60 or $70 very fast if there is a turn for the worse in its business.

Excluding Hula Hoop and similar companies, the combination of secure yield and a long-term call on the common stock of the company generally brings about a premium to the price of its convertible bond or convertible preferred stock. Such premium will depend on:

1. the "coupon," or interest rate, which is affixed to the bond (or the dividend rate set on a convertible preferred stock);
2. the proximity of the conversion price set to the existing market price of the common stock;
3. the outlook for the company itself; and
4. the general stock-market psychology at the time.

Let's assume we are considering the purchase of an original issue at $100 of a 5-percent convertible and generalize as closely as possible what we might expect in the way of market price depending on the 3 and 4 factors (i.e., company prospects and general market psychology). The table on page 88, which constitutes our Profit-Aid 15, gives you these price ranges, in each case assuming that the yield is within one-half to one percent of what a nonconvertible issue of the same company would return and assuming the conversion price is set about fifteen percent above the existing price of the company's common stock.

This table gives you a range of prices which might be expected on convertibles being issued originally at $100. As you can see, the convertibles of the very encouraging companies can be expected to jump to immediate premiums. By the same token, convertibles in very good general markets likewise command a premium price. But suppose you are unable to purchase these convertibles on their original terms at $100; suppose instead you are considering the purchase of one which has already risen to a premium. Should you buy it at these inflated levels? What are your possible risks and rewards from here?

Let's return to our XYZ bond, which is convertible into ten shares of common stock, which is now selling at $8.50 in

General Market Psychology	Public Opinion of the Company's Progress	Price of Convertible Which Might Be Expected
Extremely strong	Extremely encouraging	$115–130
Extremely strong	Good	110–120
Extremely strong	Fair	100–110
Extremely strong	Poor	95–100
Good	Extremely encouraging	110–120
Good	Good	105–115
Good	Fair	100–105
Good	Poor	90–100
Fair	Extremely encouraging	105–115
Fair	Good	103–108
Fair	Fair	100–103
Fair	Poor	90–100
Poor	Extremely encouraging	100–110
Poor	Good	100–105
Poor	Fair	90–100
Poor	Poor	85–100

the market. Assume we have a good market and that XYZ is viewed as a good growth company in investment circles. From our table above, we might find XYZ convertible selling in the $105–115 price range because of the bond's safety of income and because its conversion feature provides a chance to share in the company's future. If the bond sells at $110, the stock has to rise over the years to $11 to justify paying its current price (ten shares of common at $11 per share = $110). In actual practice the bond will usually stay ahead of its mathematical conversion value; in the case of the common rising from $8.50 to $11.00 (a twenty-nine percent increase), the bond will probably rise from $110 to $120 or so (an approximate ten-percent increase). Thus, while the downside risk of buying XYZ convertible bond even at the premium price of $110 was probably less than buying the common stock outright, the upside potentials are lessened somewhat by the premium paid. The reason that the downside risk in buying the bond is less than buying the common outright is that the former will generally remain at its "established" premium (or at least within a few points) even if the stock drops off fairly far. In our XYZ example, the stock might drop from $8.50 to, say, $6.00 (a twenty-nine-percent decline), and chances are the bond will continue to sell within ten percent or so of the $110 price.

To trace this further, let's suppose XYZ common actually has declined to $6.00 and the XYZ convertible bond has dropped back to $100. Now what risks and rewards exist? One thing above all is apparent: that XYZ common will have to show a whopping advance to make the convertible very profitable. I said before that an $11 price on XYZ common would cause the convertible to sell at about $120. Therefore, a rise from $6 to $11—an eighty-three-percent increase—in the common brings about a rise from $100 to $120—a twenty-percent increase—in the bonds. Thus, unless you have very little invested capital in the bonds (unless you have leveraged yourself with heavy borrowing, which can be accomplished with bonds), you should consider buying the *stock* at $6.00 instead of the bond at $100—if capital gain is your goal.

Don't think this XYZ example is just theory. It is completely typical of many convertible bonds and/or preferred stocks on the market today. A perfect illustration of this involves the convertible bonds of Baxter Laboratories, which were brought to market for the first time in 1962. These 4-percent bonds carried a twenty-year life, to mature in 1982, and they gave their owners the right to convert them into Baxter common stock at $38.00 per share. When the bonds were first issued, Baxter common was selling around $33.00; thus, the five-dollar differential between the market price of the common and the $38.00 conversion price was just a shade over fifteen percent. The general market was poor at the time these bonds were first issued; the outlook for Baxter was extremely encouraging. And just as our table on page 88 shows, the bonds immediately traded in the $103–108-range and "settled" for a while around $106. Just about that time the stock

market weakened further and Baxter common declined from
$33.00 to as low as around $21.00. Interestingly, the Baxter
convertible bonds did not fall with the common and were still
$104–105. The general market then turned around and Bax-
ter shot up to $27.50. And what happened to the bonds? They
rose only to $109! And it would no doubt take another sharp
move upward in Baxter common—perhaps to $33 or so—to
move these bonds much above $109.

So you can see that you get what you pay for. You may
feel more secure buying a convertible bond, even at a small
premium, because you see limited downside risk. But your
percentage gains may also be correspondingly low. And remember that I said "small premium." When you pay a large
premium you are taking more risk than you think. A lot depends, of course, on the outlook for the company in which
you are investing. Personally I never feel secure paying $120
for a convertible like XYZ when the stock is $6.00 or $7.00
or even $8.00. Because, if the company's overall outlook
changes (even if this "change" is just a figment in the investors' minds) and the stock turns weaker, the convertible can
easily drop well below $100. If you pay $100 or $105 for it
at the beginning, then it's not so bad, but when you pay $120
your percentage loss of capital looms much larger.

Let me repeat that the "proper price" to pay for a convertible depends greatly on the company's outlook. And let me
say that you should be willing to pay more of a premium for
the convertible of a company whose stock pays little or nothing in the way of dividends. In this case, investors know that
they get no return (yield) from the common stock and they
see this convertible as the one way of getting income from
this company's securities and also getting a chance to share in
its future growth.

Lastly, I would be remiss if I failed to mention the leverage
possibilities inherent in owning convertibles. In short, an investor can secure much greater borrowing power (from
banks and other lending institutions) on convertible bonds
which are listed on the New York Stock Exchange than on

common stocks.* If a person only puts up $25 of his own money on the purchase of a $100 bond (and borrows the remaining $75), the bond need not move as much as the common to show a handsome return on the owner's equity; thus, the $100 bond going up just $5 to $105 gives the borrowed owner a twenty-percent gain on his invested capital ($5 gain on $25 capital = 20 percent). Needless to say, this kind of leverage works both ways—and, as stated, convertibles can drop in price, too (especially those of lower-quality companies).

I am hopeful that most of the mysteries of convertible securities have now been cleared up. The risks and rewards should now be apparent to you, and the utilization of Profit-Aid 15, on page 88, should be of great value to you if you are considering the purchase and sale of convertibles over the years.

---

* At this time, there is the distinct possibility that such borrowing will be outlawed by the Federal Reserve Board. In this case, the price ranges of convertible securities as shown in Profit-Aid 15 would have to be lowered—by about five percent.

Chapter Twelve

How to Be Prepared
for the Unexpected

In the last decade, as in every decade, there have been a number of serious "bolts from the blue" which have caused serious, although temporary, declines in the stock market. President Eisenhower's heart attack (1955), the sudden Cuban crisis in 1962, and the tragic assassination of President Kennedy in 1963 were three such events which "threw the market for a loop" and created near-panic situations on the various stock exchanges, as well as the over-the-counter market. In the case of the happenings involving both President Eisenhower and President Kennedy, the news brought about almost unbelievable weakness—in each case causing the Dow Jones Industrial Average to fall *over thirty points*. In both events it was not unusual to see individual stocks lose as much as twenty to forty percent of their market values in just one day. Yes, *twenty to forty percent in one day!*

Certainly the events which precipitated the declines were shocking, and yet I do not think I am using only hindsight to say that *losses of such proportions are hardly ever deserved*. As a matter of fact, barring all-out war, I cannot think of any one event which by itself should really cause values to be reduced at once by percentages as high as those just mentioned. As a matter of fact, in many cases the event which creates the extreme emotionalism ends up having exactly opposite implications in the stock market. The Cuban crisis was just such an example. After the United States flexed its muscles and stood up to the Russians—and was successful—the country's stature was so much improved that both the economy and investor confidence received a significant "shot in the arm." And, from this, the stock market commenced its dramatic recovery of 1963.

Oddly enough, the death of President Kennedy also had opposite implications on the market. From a completely objective viewpoint, the inauguration of a new President (Johnson) actually took the market higher than it was before the assassination. This is not in the form of any criticism of John F. Kennedy; I am only repeating what the history books will show. Mr. Kennedy had a decidedly more "liberal" image than that of his successor (the administration's attitude toward the steel companies and their pricing policies in 1962 had been one of a number of causes for the drastic 1962 market crash); furthermore, just prior to Mr. Kennedy's death, his ambitious and all-important tax-cut program appeared to be losing steam in Congress—and the death brought about almost a public mandate for its passage.

At any rate, I think you can see that the severe market weakness in the cases of both Cuba and the death of President Kennedy turned out to be completely unwarranted. And, obviously, anyone who was fortunate enough to have purchased securities on those days of panic in the market was handsomely rewarded for his alertness.

How many people do you know, however, who actually made purchases on these days of panic? Very few, if any, I would guess! And why? Simply because few people had the time to act (the market on the day of President Kennedy's assassination was halted within about an hour of the news release), or few people had the foresight to recognize what might evolve from the disaster, or few people had the fortitude to fight the crowd and take a buying position. Emotion was at its peak, and it was indeed difficult to be rational.

As already mentioned, losses of the proportions mentioned are hardly ever deserved—which is another way of saying that an investor should divorce himself from his emotions and actually act directly contrary to such first reactions. This is really a cardinal rule in the stock market.

But, being human, sometimes we need something to force us into taking correct actions—and so we come to Profit-Aid 16. This Aid *involves the use of open buy orders for a handful of stocks.* This advice, if followed, is bound to bring the wrath of every stockbroker in the country upon me (because of the added paperwork involved)—but I only wish I had followed the advice myself in the past five years. Suppose, for example, I had placed three or four open orders to buy some quality stocks twenty to thirty percent below their existing prices. These orders would have cost me nothing (and, of course, they could have been revoked by me at any time prior to their execution). But their existence would have made an objective, unemotional, shrewd investor out of me—and in each case the purchases made would have brought me a twenty-to-thirty-percent profit in but a matter of days.

Needless to say, a person should never place such open orders if he doesn't have the money available to pay for the purchases. But if one is liquid and has the buying power, why shouldn't he be prepared for the unexpected and know that he stands a great chance of profiting from same if and when it ever occurs? Obviously the answer is: "He should!"—and this is the reasoning behind Profit-Aid 16.

Chapter Thirteen

How to Amass Large Amounts of Capital

I suppose it would be more glamorous if I had entitled the above "How to Amass a Fortune," rather than merely "Large Amounts of Capital." I avoided this, both because the use of the word "fortune" carries a connotation (to me) of promotion and because, let us face it, not everyone can expect to end up with a fortune. (What, exactly, is a fortune anyway?) In other words, I am only trying to be conservative and do not want to promise you anything which may not be attainable.

Despite this conservatism, let me make it quite clear that I believe that anyone who either starts with some capital and/or who has the dedication to save some dollars (and invest same) over the years *can* accumulate *very large sums*.

Needless to say, all parts of this book are intended to prepare you for this very goal; you should become an accomplished, sophisticated investor and thus have the skills necessary to make *and keep* substantial assets. Most important, your reading should provide you with both the methods *and the philosophy* which have to be an integral part of your stock-market "arsenal."

Italicizing the word "philosophy" was intentional, mainly because it is my belief that this is what separates the proverbial men from the boys in the battle for real success. In short, there are countless investors who have all the tools required to succeed but who never seem to click the way they should. It is my contention that the one thing lacking in the vast majority of instances is proper thought process, proper understanding—proper philosophy.

I like to think that this kind of philosophy exists throughout this whole book; indeed, if you come away from your reading with no more than a logical, sensible (*common sense*) approach to investing, then we have both succeeded. But now to the more specific question at hand: How to amass large amounts of capital.

Let me start out by listing a few basic rules which have been touched upon already, but which bear repetition, such as:

1. The big money made in the stock market comes from *investing*—as opposed to *trading*. The trader, by definition, takes his profits and runs and by so doing precludes himself from the stocks which quadruple, quintuple, etc. In addition, the trader has both commission costs and taxes working against him.
2. The wise investor builds himself a foundation of top companies located in the most attractive industries *before he starts dillydallying around*.
3. Once he is ready for special-situation investing, the smart buyer emphasizes the companies which hold the prospect of multiplying capital many times over the years—as opposed to the twenty-five-to-fifty-percent type of goal.

Naturally, these three hints are but scratching the surface —but they formulate the basis for the aforementioned philosophy which I deem all-important. Inherent in all three are:

patience and tenacity—the simple ability *to hang on*. This is not to say a person should become unalterably wedded to his securities or that I am opposed to taking profits in stocks. The preceding (and succeeding) chapters will school you in this very buy-sell procedure. But I should make it clear that the *inability to accumulate large sums* (yes, even fortunes) *usually stems from an inability to stand prosperity*. Think of how many people there must be who *sold* Xerox at $10 or $20; or Polaroid at similar levels. In each case, a $10,000 sold investment would be worth between $200,000 and $300,000 today. And while your definition of a large amount of money may be more than this, certainly an individual does not need more than a few of these accumulations to live the way he wants for the rest of his life.

Naturally, there are many considerations involved in both the original selection of a Xerox or a Polaroid and in the purchase and retention of same. The purpose of this chapter, however, goes beyond the reaches of security analysis. Instead, it entails an extension of the philosophy of hanging on and provides a tool for achieving the home runs as opposed to the bunt singles.

Let us start by understanding the integral parts of stock investing: What and When to buy; and What and When to sell. Goodness knows, volumes and volumes have been written on these subjects—and this book covers the points, too. To summarize and repeat, we know that What to buy means fine, well-managed companies operating in attractive fields; and that When to buy means relating the kind of progress anticipated—the eventual fundamentals of the companies— to the present market price. And we know that the What and When to sell are no more than an extension of the same processes: What stage of maturity are the various companies and industries in and how do the resulting profit projections relate to market prices?

Apparently—and this a crucial point to consider—the ability to buy stocks is much better developed than the ability to sell. Why, though? Why are there so many people who had the wisdom to purchase Xerox and Polaroid, but who lacked the vision to hold them for the big, big gain? Here is where I intend to do some exploration for you—and to arrive at a thinking process which should enable you to become a better holder of securities for the huge rewards.

In our psychoanalysis of "stupidity in selling," we should understand our not always consistent mental processes. Very consistent and understandable is the fear of loss. It is hardly easy to buy a stock and immediately see your capital being drained as it is if your timing is a bit off and the stock sinks soon after purchase. All we can do to overcome this is to emphasize the importance of patience. Some stocks will take time to develop. Either the fundamentals take longer to develop than anticipated or the investment community may not catch on to the attractiveness of the stock or the industry as soon as you might like. Alas, Rome was not built in a day. And patience is, indeed, a virtue.

Believe it or not, many people become even more nervous when their stock has risen (especially if it has been a rapid ascent) than when they have a loss. A person may be able to "live" with a loss merely because he is the procrastinator type who shuts his eyes to reality, who refuses to look at failure, or simply rationalizes same (and thus can live with a loss). At any rate, experience has shown that the very person who can adjust to a loss may have one heck of a time living with a profit. I suppose it is the conservation element in many: once we have something in hand, we hate to see it slip away.

There are other, very practical inhibitions which hamper investors from staying around for the grand coup. One is the indoctrination that "No one ever went broke taking a profit." Certainly this is true and we all know the Wall Street adage about hogs never making money in the market. As mentioned, however, if we continuously engage in selling securities we will never achieve the Xerox-Polaroid results.

A second obstacle to overcome has, unfortunately, to do with stockbrokers themselves. Let's face it, a broker is not a charitable institution and he is going to have a hard time making money off an account which is completely inactive. I realize I am skating on thin ice here, and no doubt every broker in the country will hate me for even broaching the subject. Let me make it clear that I am not accusing the profession of churning accounts or of doing anything harmful by design. But there is a gray area in which it takes the most idealistic broker to deter a client from pitching out a security on which he has made a handsome profit. This is true if for no other reason than the fickleness of the market itself. In short, anything can happen in the stock market (and usually does), and everyone having witnessed riches-to-rags stocks (as everyone has) is bound to be influenced by such experiences. In other words, the broker who keeps his client from selling a stock in which the latter may be nervous to begin with is placing his head on a potential chopping block.

So it takes a broker who is not desperately hungry (thereby not needing every commission possible to exist) or one who has a real belief in the security in question—to calm the client down and say, "Let your profit ride. Stay where you are."

Enough of this psychological examination, however. It is time to get to the issue at hand (how to amass large amounts of capital) and attack it from a positive viewpoint. In so doing, let me make it clear that I am addressing myself to those interested in accumulating *large* amounts of capital. I am not advocating that everyone try to accomplish this; it is too easy to succeed without speculating and without going for the huge profits simply through buying and holding consistent (albeit not spectacular) securities and letting them compound themselves over the years.

We have, however, made the assumption that quite a number of investors are motivated toward the larger "killings," and we would be remiss if we did not help these people along with the others. But how? How can we ever aid this group which is desirous of achieving the big numbers?

The answer, as I will present it, is going to be quite simple. It is going to entail an approach, rather than any formulas or any complicated procedures which are bound to be useless in the vast majority of cases. In other words, each individual security is going to present its own problems of analysis and it is unrealistic to generalize—except on a philosophical basis. So now we are ready to complete the circle and finish what we have started. Remember—we commenced by indicating how many people have unhappily sold out of Xerox and Polaroid and the like over the years and how the big money is made through the accumulation of but a few winners in your lifetime. So let us carry it one step further and literally force ourselves into having the proper perspective and the proper patience to wait out the market and be holders, not sellers, of the real growth companies.

Oddly enough, pure security analysis hardly provides you with this ability. As a matter of fact, the more fundamentally oriented (that is, the more you are keyed to stock selection based on low multiples of earnings), the less able you may be to hang on to companies which have great futures but which may get ahead of themselves in market price—as they are prone to do.

The answer, to repeat, lies in an approach—one which gives you the aforementioned perspective and patience. This approach, like so many successful ones in life, evolves from setting proper *goals*. Indeed, it is a method of goal-setting which can enable you to supervise your portfolio of stocks correctly—and to be able to live with the prosperity of the Xerox-Polaroid type of investments.

Let me develop this thinking by utilizing, as example, the simplest kind of goal—that of achieving very modest gains over the years from one's investments. If you are a conservative investor, one who cannot take risks, then you buy securities for a combination of stable (and, hopefully, steadily growing) income and enough market appreciation to offset inflation and whatever growing needs develop. In such cases, you buy stocks without illusions of grandeur and *you are satisfied if your income rises each year and if your stocks achieve some modest appreciation as time goes by*. In short, your goals have been set and you learn to be happy with your investments so long as there is evidence that these goals are being achieved. In looking over your list periodically, you consider each stock within this framework and you retain the companies which are apparently making some kind of progress. In other words, your goals are modest and you must be satisfied with modest performance.

But what about the growth-seeking investor, the one whose goals are not so modest? Most probably he has diversified his portfolio with a number of securities (hopefully not too many!), with individual stocks having varying degrees of profit potential. He may have a growth-type utility stock, in which his goals are set for ten-to-fifteen-percent annual growth (on average); he may have an Eastman Kodak, a Warner-Lambert, a Union Oil, and/or other industrial companies in which he envisions similar (ten-to-fifteen-percent) increments; and he may have an Avon, a Bristol-Myers, an IBM, and a Polaroid-Xerox in which he has greater things in mind.

The important consideration here involves his seeing his investments as a Big Picture. If he bought Bristol-Myers or Litton or IBM or Xerox or Polaroid as *foundation stocks* (i.e., bought them to *own* them, not to pitch them out for small profit), he should not lose sight of this goal. The fact that one or more of these might have jumped fifty percent or so in market price in the past year should not create panic, but instead should produce satisfaction in that the stocks are doing what they are intended to do.

This is not to say that one should be blind to what is going on around him and that anyone should shut his eyes to fundamentals, excessive speculative activity in the market, or industry conditions and corporate developments. The biggest mistake made by *former* owners of great growth companies, however, has been their propensity for trying to be too smart. The person who conjectures that his stock is too high because it has gone from twenty to twenty-five times earnings is probably trying to be too smart (provided, of course, that the company is still progressing).

Repeating that I do not favor a "hear-no-evil, see-no-evil" attitude, I have found one approach (an extension of all of the above) which keeps *me* from being "too smart." The approach (Profit-Aid 17) goes something like this:

1. I try to categorize each stock I buy or own according to its characteristics. Is it a cyclical-type company which will have to be sold at some time? Is it a gradual-growth equity? Is it a rank speculation? Or is it a reliable-type, fast-growth equity?
2. From the above, I determine just how much of a position I would be happy with in the future in each stock.
3. In supervising my list, I give heavy weight to both the category and the ultimate-exposure approaches—*even more weight than I do in determining exactly what kind of price-earnings multiple might be "perfect" for it.*

Let's take the case of buying or holding IBM stock. Immediately I categorize this as a high-quality, fast-growth situation. Going to Step 2, I determine that I could live happily with a heavy position in IBM; in other words, I could sleep nights knowing I had a large amount of money in this company. Then I look at the stock with these thoughts in mind. I find that it is selling for forty times this year's anticipated earnings, and of course I determine whether any severe interruption of its growth pattern is in store. Assuming that the latter (fundamental-company) position is still promising, *I relax with my holding.* I do *not* look at it with a supermagnifying glass and place an arbitrary multiple on the stock and, finding that the market's assessment is slightly higher than mine, sell it out. I adhere to the Big Picture approach, which is the longer-term approach, which tells me to be happy that I have a large profit in a high-quality, fast-growth company in which I *want* a large position anyway.

Thus, provided I have done my homework correctly at the beginning by satisfying myself that both industry and company prospects are encouraging, I feel secure with what will probably continue to amaze me over the years. Time flies by and today's higher-than-anticipated P/E multiple will be reduced considerably by the fast-growing company's progress.

Needless to say, this kind of approach is incorrect in the assessment of cyclical stocks or in ones which may be here today and gone tomorrow or in ones which (e.g., Chapter 1's example of the bowling equities) are approaching maturity or market deterioration.

I said at the beginning that the meat of this chapter would be philosophical. It certainly has been that, but this does not mean that it lacks usefulness. I will repeat over and over that the key to success in the stock market emanates from a good deal of common sense, and of course philosophy is an integral part of this. As mentioned, there is no fancy formula presented here, but your understanding of the approach and your ability to set proper goals will do as much for you over the years as all the formulas combined.

Chapter Fourteen

How to Separate Attractive from Unattractive Industries

Certainly any instruction on How to Make Money in the Stock Market should dwell on separating attractive from unattractive investments. That is, as they say, "the name of the game," and I have already indicated that the key to attractive and/or unattractive *investments* revolves around separating attractive from unattractive *industries*.

Actually, we have already explored this all-important area —starting with the foresight approach in Chapter 1 and going on to the explanation of pendulum patterns in Chapter 2, the importance of product differentiation in Chapter 3, a checklist of questions to be posed in industry analysis in Chapter 5 (page 43), and numerous references to the subject in practically every other chapter. Furthermore, the Appendix provides you with an Industry-Rating Guide, which goes a long way in pinpointing attractive industries and distinguishing them from the less-attractive and the downright unattractive.

Despite this coverage, I feel it essential to go further and

104

make as much a professional out of you as I can. And since actual examples are always more meaningful than theory, I am going to utilize the example approach. Most of the major business schools in this country emphasize the case method of instruction, and this is precisely the method we will be using.

Sometimes the most effective teaching is done by going to extremes, and thus I am going to start with a discussion of metal stocks—which I deem unattractive from a consistent, long-range standpoint. From there, I will compare the metals with another group—in this case, the papers (which I consider only moderately interesting). And then I will close with a thesis on the proprietary-drug stocks—which I consider extremely attractive. Most important, the comparisons of these three fields should give you better insight into proper thought process and thereby prepare you to separate attractive from unattractive industries.

Let's start now with discussion of the metals and see whether they look to be bright or tarnished.

In Chapter 3's list of nondifferentiated products, I placed various metals under the category *lacking* uniqueness; in the great, great majority of cases, this is the very category into which metals belong. This is, however, only one of many points to be analyzed, so we will commence on a thorough, objective appraisal of the group. Perhaps the most effective approach is to weigh the pros and cons of the industry, and this is just what I intend to do for you now.

On the optimistic side are the following points:

1. Metals are basic to the economy. Autos, airplanes, tractors, buildings, heavy construction of all types, machine tools, ships, trains, all have as their base: metal. In other words, the economy cannot survive without it.
2. Some important technological advances have been made in recent years in metal production and fabrication—all of which has served to lower break-even points for most manufacturers.
3. The metal industry requires substantial sums for origi-

nal investment, thereby eliminating the risk of many new entries into the business. By the same token, metal companies need large natural resources to conduct their business, and these resources are generally very hard to find and require considerable funds and technological know-how to convert into the end product.

On the pessimistic side, we find these:

1. Metals generally are being subjected to challenges from nonmetallic substances, such as plastics.
2. The metals are constantly fighting among themselves for markets (i.e., aluminum vs. steel vs. copper).
3. Certain technological advances by the metal industry are actually reducing the amounts of metals used (i.e., new method for producing tin cans with less tinplate— to cut down weight and cost—means less steel used).
4. The major industries served by metals are: (a) construction; (b) consumer durable goods; and (c) industrial equipment—all of which are cyclical in nature.
5. Metal companies generally have heavy fixed overhead charges. In an effort to spread out these overhead charges, the companies tend to overproduce, thereby creating an unfavorable supply-and-demand relationship in their field.
6. Labor problems have proved disruptive.
7. Price is the buyer's paramount consideration because there is little or no difference between the product offered by one company vs. that of another. Because of this lack of differentiation, foreign imports are a threat.
8. The metal industry as a whole has a hard time justifying price increases, because higher prices on one metal invite the usage of competing metals and materials.
9. Scrap metal can be utilized by certain users, thereby eliminating some new-metal purchases.

Naturally it is dangerous to generalize about an industry with so many different facets. To be completely fair, we should really separate the older metals—those which are at "maturity" in that their growth will coincide more with population increases rather than increased usage on a per-capita basis—with the newer metals. The older group, which has to include copper, lead, steel, zinc, and others, is fighting to protect existing markets and thus is certainly subject to all the pessimistic thoughts advanced above. The common stocks of companies involved with these metals lack inherent growth and should be bought only by those who want to trade cyclical issues and/or those who want the above-average yield these stocks usually provide. As long-term capital-gain vehicles, these stocks leave much to be desired.

The newer metals, which include aluminum, nickel, and various low-tonnage participants such as platinum, cadmium, beryllium, etc., look more glamorous. In most cases, these metals hold promise of showing increased per-capita consumption over the near term and thus may not have all the drawbacks I listed for the overall group. Despite this, I have a hard time getting enthused over their long-term prospects, too. Basically, they still "fit the mold" I advanced for the whole metal field. If they are at all exempt, chances are very great that the exemption will be short-lived. History has proved that metals, like human beings, do not grow forever. It is one thing to invest in a metal which is in its earlier stages and which has great growth ahead of it; it is another to expect this growth to continue for very long. In addition, the investor should be aware of the great risks in the new "glamour-metal" business. In the mid-1950's everyone was enchanted with the prospects for titanium, the new "wonder metal," but profitability was slow in coming and is not significant today. In the late 1950's beryllium became a magic word, but look and see how much money the beryllium companies have made so far. Also—very little! Likewise, the whole 1950–1960 decade was one of talk about aluminum and its fantastic prospects. At the beginning of this period aluminum stocks were selling at three to six times earnings, and the early investors made huge sums because the public glamorized the group and took these stocks to forty times earnings. But all that glitters is not gold—or aluminum—or any other metal. Despite increased consumption, the earnings records of these companies from 1955 and 1956 through 1962 were extremely disappointing. Long-term holders of these stocks lost money over this period—despite a generally rising stock market.

Steel vs. Paper

When considering stocks for investment, you have many different industries from which you can choose. Throughout this book I have attempted to give you my reasons for being attracted or for being discouraged about the prospects for certain groups. When doing so, I am trying to accomplish two things, namely: (a) to show you specifically where I think your dollars should be invested, so that you will maximize your results; and (b) to train you to think in a sensible, logical, objective manner, which will make you a more flexible and more accomplished investor. It is this latter aim which prompts me now to discuss the investment merits of steel and paper. As you will see, I am not concerned with making a strong argument for investing in paper stocks, nor do I believe they deserve such recommendation. My purpose in selecting paper here is to show you how industries can be somewhat similar in nature and yet, when a real appraisal is made, how one has such strong advantages over the other that you wonder how anyone could come to anything other than one decision.

Steel and paper are unlike in appearance and use, but both are basic to our economy. Both businesses entail large capital investment and substantial natural resources, thereby eliminating the small operator. Both are sensitive to general economic conditions and both have large fixed overhead expenses which have to be met regardless of business. Both have a certain level of operation which breaks them even and both reap fat profits when these capacity levels are exceeded by much. And both, for the most part, have nondifferentiated products.

But now to the important differences between these two basic materials—differences which would automatically come to you if you forced yourself into objective thinking. One significant difference involves the usage of steel and paper, the former going into fairly permanent and indestructible objects while the latter (paper) is expendable and is used up and destroyed almost immediately. This, of course, means that there is a strong replacement demand for paper, and as long as competing materials do not invade the markets (plastics, for example, are replacing certain usages once dominated by paper products), this replacement demand should be more reliable than the original products which steel makes.

The existence of scrap steel and scrap paper likewise poses different problems in these two large industries. Steel scrap comes back to "haunt" the manufacturers, in that it is used by many companies in place of new steel. On the other hand, paper scrap does not go back into its original form. Wastepaper is converted into cartons and other paper products, but it is not put back into its original state. Thus, the companies which are strong in paper itself and are not heavily involved in container board are not hampered by this scrap situation.

Labor costs of the two industries are also different. Labor accounts for approximately thirty percent of sales in the paper industry, whereas wages and other labor expenses represent about thirty-eight percent of steel sales. In an economy which is well tied to the principle of steadily rising labor costs, this gives the paper industry a definite plus over the steel group.

Most important, and certainly indicative of relative industry strengths, is the trend of paper and steel consumption on a per-person basis in this country. Over the 1955–1964 decade, for example, the per-capita consumption was as follows:

Pounds Per Capita

	1955*	1964*	Increase
Paper	422*	478	13.3%
Steel	857*	917	7.0

* Due to volatility of steel consumption, I have taken an average figure for the years 1955–1959 as a base. Source: American Iron & Steel Institute, "Charting Steel's Progress During 1964," p. 34. I have also used the 1955–1959 average as the base for paper. Source: Standard & Poor's Industry Surveys, "Paper," p. P–7.

In addition, steel has been subject to a more serious trend of competition from foreign production. Imports of the metal practically doubled over the 1960–1964 span, while paper experienced an increase of just eight and one-half percent.

There are many other factors which could be brought out to prove why there are fewer problems in the paper field than in steel. Once again let me say that this is not intended to present a strong bullish argument for paper shares. The consumer-paper companies such as Scott have certainly outperformed any steel company I can think of, but the paper group as a whole has been unable to withstand cyclical fluctuations in the economy.

In addition, price-cutting has been typical of paper, whereas steel has been quite "well disciplined" in this respect. Nonetheless, investors have been more conscious of the relative advantages of paper—and the market has responded by assigning higher P/E multiples to this group than to the steels. To illustrate, the latter have sold in the eight-to-twelve-times range over the past decade, compared with fifteen to twenty times for the papers.

To repeat, I am not suggesting that papers are undervalued. Nor am I saying that the steels cannot have their day in the future; as a matter of fact, what with the steel industry spending about two billion dollars a year on plant modernization and improvement, it is my impression that the next cyclical upturn in our economy will point up some unusual earnings for the major steel companies. This latent bullishness is, however, of a cyclical nature and it has to be considered in the context of our discussions in chapters 7 and 19.

The purpose of this case study of steel and paper has been explained: to improve your analytical approach. Now let us go on and relate these two industries to one in which I have great conviction—and which will serve as a fine illustration of how to think the right way in common-stock selection.

Proprietary Drugs

I am referring to the business of proprietary drugs (proprietary drugs being those which are sold over-the-counter, without prescription—as opposed to so-called ethical, prescription drugs). Perhaps the best approach in relating this industry to steel and paper is to compare some of the more basic characteristics discussed previously. Such comparison stacks up as follows:

1. Whereas paper and steel are sensitive to the general economy, drugs (ethical *and* proprietary) are not; indeed, the latter might be termed "recession resistant."
2. Demand factors are clearly more favorable for the proprietary-drug industry. Per-capita consumption (as shown on page 110) showed but modest increase for paper and steel over the 1955–1964 span (13.3 and 7.0 percent, respectively). Over the same period, retail sales of proprietary medicines went from 1.2 billion to 1.9 billion dollars, for an increase of almost sixty percent, and per-capita figures grew approximately thirty-six percent. While these statistics are not directly comparable, the disparity is quite obvious.
3. Drugs are, of course, highly consumable.
4. The labor factor in the drug industry generally (including both ethical and proprietary) is very low, i.e., approximately twenty-seven percent, as compared with the thirty-to-thirty-eight-percent range for paper-steel.
5. Proprietary drugs are very much differentiated; they are hardly commodity-type items.
6. The proprietary-drug industry is the classical example

of firm price structure. I have always contended that consumers are neither terribly aware of price differences when they are shopping for proprietaries, nor do they base their purchase decisions on the price element. As a matter of fact, a psychological study would no doubt prove that we feel better paying *more* for a product we are buying to alleviate an ailment (this is different in the case of nonprescription *vs.* prescription: the doctor is prescribing the latter and the use of generic drugs by him in no way affects your attitude).

The records of the top-flight proprietary-drug outfits has left little to be desired. A short time ago I compiled the results of six such companies* for both the 1956–1965 decade and for the single year 1966. The ten-year span for the six companies obviously meant that sixty figures were utilized and the results showed that in *only one instance* out of the sixty was there a decline in profits from the previous year (and this one case involved a dip of one penny per share). Furthermore, the ten-year figures showed that the smallest average *annual* gain in earnings was eight percent, running up to eighteen percent compounded annually for the fastest growing of the six. And 1966 actually showed an acceleration of this trend, what with one company experiencing an eleven-percent increase, four companies fifteen-to-twenty-percent growth, and one registering a thirty-five-percent gain.

In my comparison of paper and steel, I indicated that the main purpose was to school you in the correct thought process. My mention of the proprietary-drug industry, of course, has the same goal—although I must be frank and tell you that the discussion has additional value. In short, if you have never considered ownership in this group, it is my contention that you should! In addition, awareness of the strengths of a group such as this ties in well with the philosophical approach developed in Chapter 13. These stocks, while not explosive like the Xerox-Polaroid variety, constitute the kind which

* American Home Products, Bristol-Myers, Norwich, Plough, Sterling, and Warner-Lambert.

should be viewed for their Big Picture—which is another way
of saying that they should remain as strong building blocks
for amassing large amounts of capital. They may look somewhat out of line at times on a P/E-multiple basis, but they
should produce sufficient results over the years so that the
holder of them should not be too cute or too smart—and
eliminate them because they look a bit too high for the
moment.

Part Two

Protecting Yourself Against Costly Mistakes in the Market

Chapter Fifteen

You, Grass Roots, and Investing

Many people believe that the stock market is only for the professionals—for those persons who have considerable time and some secret skills to fathom the mysteries of such investing. While security analysis is a science (of sorts) which requires a knowledge of accounting, statistics, etc., there are certain elements of this vocation which are completely devoid of technical skills. In fact, it is my personal opinion that it is these *non*technical skills which "make or break" the analyst. I further contend that you—a "nonprofessional"—can make successful decisions based on certain of these nontechnical factors. Indeed, correct use of the nontechnical considerations will most often outperform strict usage of the technical aspects.

What I am trying to say is that you, too, can become a fine judge of stock values and correspondingly become a fine judge of what to buy and what not to buy.

For example, you don't have to be an analyst to utilize the all-important foresight I emphasized in Chapter 1. Nor do you have to hold any college degrees or have knowledge of balance sheets and income statements to accomplish a second important nontechnical approach to investing which I will now explain.

This second clue is very simple and very obvious. But so was the invention of the safety pin—and so are many money-making schemes and products. So don't guffaw when you hear me instruct you to approach your prospective investments from the lowest levels—from the grass roots.

Let me show you what I mean.

I'm sure you are aware of the existence throughout the country of the professional security analysts (now called "financial analysts") I mentioned above. These men (and women) spend their time seeking out attractive situations. If you asked the typical analyst how he spends his time, his answer would be something like the following:

X percent of my time reading about the industry or industries that I follow.

X percent of my time talking to corporate officials either by phone or by personal visit.

X percent of my time talking to security salesmen in our office.

X percent of my time exchanging ideas with other analysts.

What is missing in this job description? What else should this typical analyst be doing to be better prepared to make the right decisions? My answer is that he should spend a good deal of time "just moseying around"—right down on the grass-roots level. An automobile analyst, for example, should set aside time to check what is happening at the retail level. He should determine what kind of floor traffic the auto dealers are experiencing, because any experienced dealer will tell you that this day-to-day traffic is one of the best indicators of how long and how well the new cars will sell. This doesn't mean he can judge from the success of one dealer and this fellow's attitude. Instead, the analyst should get a good cross-section view of what is going on.

Likewise, you can learn a lot about where the auto industry is trending by determining the grass-roots climate in the used-car business. I'm sure you know that used-car prices have a direct bearing on new-car sales. After all, the great percentage of cars sold are in exchange for the buyer's old car; if used-car prices in general are firm, then the dealer has more "room" to make an attractive deal on his new cars and more people are enticed into buying. This important factor is available to you as well as to the professional security analyst; indeed, it is really a layman's statistic and is easily obtained.

By the same token, the cosmetics analysts should get down to the consumer level to come to a fair conclusion of a company's competitive position. I well remember my own experience with Helene Curtis stock. I had become attracted to this company in 1961, mainly because of some earnings projections secured by some New York analyst friends of mine. Their contact had been directly with Curtis management and, of course, this was bound to be somewhat prejudiced. Rather than rely solely on this information, I sought out certain wholesale and retail outlets for cosmetic products. Upon doing so, I found that Helene Curtis' job of promotion and selling, as well as public acceptance of both established and new products the company had on the market, left a great deal to be desired. In short, my grass-roots approach refuted completely what had been presented to me. I placed more faith in my practical learnings than in the pure statistical presentation and forecasts and immediately contacted the few investors I knew who held Curtis stock. Fortunately all of my clients listened to the advice; all sold their stock in 1961 in the $55–60 range. I say fortunately because it was not long before the stock had declined sharply and was selling around $30 (and was trading at a mere $14 in October of 1967).

What I am emphasizing here is that certain analysts (fortunately—the minority) spend their time living in an "ivory tower." They know all there is to know about an industry or a company from twenty floors up in a skyscraper. What they fail to recognize is how much can be learned away from their tower and plush surroundings. And this, of course, is where you can do a very adequate job yourself. *You can check out an interesting story on the consumer level as well as anyone.*

There are so many other illustrations to bear this out. The bowling picture presented in Chapter 1 is typical. While certain analysts were licking their chops looking for record results for this industry for years to come, it would have taken only a few hours for a layman to conclude that the alley operators were having their problems and that this would eventually lead to a sharply lower demand for new equipment. Such few hours would certainly have been well spent when you consider what happened to Brunswick and AMF stocks.

So you can see that security analysis is not only for the "pros." By maintaining grass-roots contacts you can develop what we in the business call "good market feel." You will develop an understanding of advantages and disadvantages of certain industries and you will get to know what has a good chance for success in the market and what does not. In short, you will have developed a strong practical application to buying stocks. This practical approach plus a certain amount of arithmetic will give you what you need—and I am certain that this combination will improve your performance in the market considerably over the years.

Chapter Sixteen

"Hodgepodge" Companies:
A Fad in the Making?

Like so many men, I have had a burning interest in athletics over my lifetime. Aside from the great enjoyment I have received from this interest, I agree with those who contend that sports constitute a great teacher. Such teachings are useful in many of life's facets—including (you guessed it) the stock market. I do not intend to list all the elements of sports which can be helpful in the market, but I do see one analogy which I think will help to prove an important point.

Thinking back over the years, I recall knowing countless men who could do many things fairly well—but who never really excelled in anything. In sports I remember so many fellows who played football in the fall, basketball in the winter, baseball in the spring, swimming and tennis in the summer. While these individuals no doubt derived great enjoyment from following this pattern, it was the great exception who excelled in any one of the above. Leaving natural ability aside, the one who made the headlines was usually the lad who concentrated in a specific area, rather than run the gamut. How many times have you read about the star pitcher or quarterback who spent countless hours—off season and on—practicing for accuracy and speed? His diligence and concentration paid off in his becoming a trained expert, and this is why he succeeded.

Indeed, this is an age of specialization—and this relates to the stock market as well as to sports and other pursuits in life. *My investment lesson here is to warn you against putting your money in companies which have no real specialty.* Just as it is a rarity to find a person who excels in all sports, it is quite unusual to find a company which becomes extremely successful in many unrelated areas.

The philosophy and discussion to follow, as well as the thesis already advanced, are very apropos at this moment—because of the widespread development (and the corresponding interest by investors) in so-called "conglomerate" companies. The conglomerates are basically buying businesses of all sorts, the theory being that a top group of executives can keep an unlimited number of "balls in the air" at the same time and run them successfully through professional management. We will explore all this in more detail later on, but before doing so we should delve into the academic approach of just how much *diversification* both an investor and a company can actually afford.

To begin with, it is my firm conviction that *investors* generally *over*diversify, thinking that a large number of stock issues will protect them from disaster. While it may well protect them from famine (it may not, too, as a long list of poorly selected securities is certainly no insurance against anything), it will also provide them with very unexciting results. Not only will a very long list of stocks generally relegate performance to mediocrity, but it will lead to laziness on the part of the investor—and laziness is just what we are trying to avoid in our approach to stock-market profits.

But back now to the subject of company selection—and to conglomerates. Just what is proper diversity of a company's business and what is imprudent spreading out?

Imagine yourself in the position of a business executive. Picture yourself trying to manage many unrelated businesses.

The problems of personnel, production, marketing, and distribution differ from business to business, so you can see that it is a mammoth job to learn the ins and outs of many different fields.

As mentioned, conglomerate mergers are the vogue of 1967, and it is my view that most such companies have basically weak underpinnings. Management might well be resorting to the accumulation of a hodgepodge of businesses for several or all of the following reasons:

1. They may well have an inflated opinion of their own managerial capabilities.
2. They may not realize that they are buying many businesses which are cyclical and which are now benefiting from record economic strength (i.e., are they prepared for inevitable cyclical downturns?).
3. They have fallen in love with the word "diversification." They think mistakenly that there is some magic to this.
4. They realize that the investing public today feels better when its companies can boast of broad diversification. In other words, management thinks that this spreading out is good for its image. (They are, of course, wrong in thinking that this will help their stock on anything but a temporary basis, because investors may recognize this overdiversification for what it is and thus the image may ultimately deteriorate because of it.)
5. They diversify on a wide basis because, either consciously or subconsciously, they are worried about the success and/or future of their basic business. This is naturally a sign of weakness and is one reason why widely diversified outfits are generally not as strong as those which stick to something they know.
6. Most probably, management is "playing the numbers game," attempting to increase per-share earnings for their company through acquisition almost without regard for long-range considerations. In so doing, they may or may not be able to justify how the addition of a new and unrelated business fits in to their operation,

and an investor should be careful to separate good business judgment from a form of rationalization.

I am sure you realize that I am not opposed to all diversification, especially to what you might call "natural diversification." For example, it was certainly natural for the major oil companies to go into the chemical business. Oil is the basis for many chemicals (petrochemicals are among the most widely used of all), and the companies would have been foolish not to convert their oil assets into an area which promised a high return on invested capital. And when certain meat companies went into sporting goods (utilizing hides), soaps (utilizing fats), and drugs (using otherwise useless animal organs), this was merely trying to get the most out of what they already had. (They say the meat producers now get "everything but the squeal from the pig.") But when a liquor company suddenly delves into unrelated chemicals, and when a small electronics-parts manufacturer enters the penicillin market, and when a general manufacturing company all of a sudden goes into the real-estate business—watch out!

In other words, you should be wary of any unrelated ventures taken. It goes without saying that the company in five, ten, or twenty different endeavors, ranging from plumbing fixtures to electronics to textiles to retailing to goodness-knows-what, is basically hodgepodge and its long-term attractiveness should, indeed, be questioned. It also seems completely logical to me that you should stick to the specialists and not be attracted by those who have only part time to devote to a given business (and who may lack the necessary knowledge to do it successfully anyway). If you think the chemical business is a growth area and you want representation, nine times out of ten you will be better off to buy Dow or another pure chemical outfit outright rather than settle for a part-time, nonspecialized operator. The same principle pertains to practically all fields.

Certainly there are exceptions to this treatment of extreme diversification. A company such as Minnesota Mining has entered a number of fields which might have looked "foreign" to its basic operations. And Litton Industries has spread itself out widely and has been exceedingly successful in doing so. Actually, a real understanding of the acquisitions made by MMM and Litton would convince you that they fit into a corporate pattern for the future. Thus, they were related to a Big Picture design. In addition, management of both companies has been truly exceptional, possessing the flexibilities and abilities to run a broadly diversified organization. And there will be more Littons and MMM's in the future. I think it is fair to conclude, however, that the more hodgepodge the conglomeration is, the tougher the road is going to be for its managerial group—which is another way of saying that diversification alone is hardly the answer, or the secret to success.

The risk involved in having all your eggs in one basket is widely publicized and accepted. We all know what happens if that one basket breaks or is dropped: all the eggs are broken and you are left with none. But is it any more protection to carry one egg in each pocket and two inside your hat? Certainly not! In fact, chances are you will have one or two eggs lost in every trip this way, so it may well prove even more dangerous than carrying them each time in one strong, well-developed basket which was intended for the purpose from the beginning.

Thus, I am telling you to beware of 1967's mad dash and enthusiasm for the conglomerates and instead, stated positively, to concentrate on companies which have a philosophy, a purpose, and a consistent direction.

Chapter Seventeen

Possibilities and Pitfalls of "Medicine-Man" Mergers

In line with the last chapter's discussion of conglomerates and, most particularly, of diversification, let's talk about the route that makes this spreading out possible: corporate marriages or, as they are called, mergers. When two companies marry, or merge, just like human beings, they consolidate their belongings under one (corporate) roof. And when this happens, there is a natural tendency for people to become enchanted with the new prospects presenting themselves. Such prospects are generally glowing; after all, these consolidations promise to eliminate duplication of production and warehousing facilities, advertising and selling efforts, personnel, etc. In other words, the cost of doing business should be reduced with the combination of the merger, as opposed to going it alone.

Like so many things, however, the theory is not the same as reality. As a matter of fact, very large mergers—which are the ones which capture the imagination of most investors— may pose problems which are difficult to overcome. Indeed, there are certain definite negatives in merging which may overrule the advantages of consolidation. Consider that:

1. Considerable expenses are necessary at the beginning simply to bring the two previously independent companies into close contact. These expenses naturally tend to reduce profits of the companies on a combined basis.
2. A certain segment of management becomes disgruntled because of the merger. After all, if the theory of elimination of duplication is correct, then the new organization will need fewer employees. Thus, right at the outset, certain employees become concerned about the mere existence of their jobs—and this does anything but good for the company morale. Likewise, many new faces are thrown together—different faces and personalities, not all of which will fit together ideally.

While mergers may look practical and encouraging on paper, I caution you against assuming that any basic sicknesses will dissolve. Think of some of the major mergers in recent years—Sperry Gyroscope and Remington Rand, for example. On paper, this might have looked like an ideal, textbook example of a to-be-successful marriage. These two seeds, crossfertilized into Sperry Rand, certainly produced no rose for the first eleven years of the combined entity. Actually, it was not until the 1966–1967 markets that Sperry Rand stock made any consistent headway.

The General Telephone-Sylvania Electric combination also looked like it fit "like a hand in a glove." General's stable telephone operations would help to support the more glamorous electronics business—and vice versa. In practice, General found it had a "bull by the tail" in Sylvania and it took a great deal of hard work and time to achieve the desired profitability. Unquestionably, General stockholders would have fared better without Sylvania in the first five years of the merger; whereas the second five years may have proved the worth of the acquisition, it may take another five to ten years to justify the complete wisdom of the move.

The marriage of the (Glenn L.) Martin Company with American Marietta is another good illustration. Of course, this to me was almost a "shotgun" affair. Why in the world would a government contractor want to enter the building-materials business, or vice versa, unless both felt quite insecure about their individual futures? Certainly the combined unit has done nothing to set the world on fire since the merger.

There are many other large mergers which go to prove that this route is but a medicine man in treating the prevailing disease. Let me emphasize, however, that I am anything but critical of totally related mergers—between two companies in related fields. For example, Chesebrough and Pond's combined forces to their great advantage, and the combined unit went on to add similar toiletry-cosmetic companies to their fold—all to the advantage of the remaining entity. Bristol-Myers made an absolute dandy of an acquisition of Clairol. Corn Products and Best Foods fit well together. Georgia-Pacific's purchase of numerous timber companies was logical "backward" integration. Beneficial Finance's buying Western Auto Supply gave it another credit-buying outlet. And countless manufacturing companies have added to their product lines in a logical extension of their basic business.

Thus, it would be foolhardy to be negative on mergers per se—and I am hardly that; as a matter of fact, "hand-in-glove" mergers intrigue me greatly. What I want you to be wary of is when two giants combine forces in what deep-thinking analysis will tell you is an effort to cure some basic ills of both parties. In other words, zero plus zero equals but zero! In a way, this is all an extension of the motto "a chain is only as strong as its weakest link." If you have a weak chain because of a weak link to begin with, adding another weak link is certainly not going to strengthen it. It will only add one more spot where the chain might break!

Chapter Eighteen

Risk-*vs.*-Reward Thinking When Speculating on Mergers and Sellouts

In line with our previous discussion of making money through corporate mergers, liquidations, and sellouts (Chapter 8), there is, to my way of thinking, one cardinal rule: *Do not be greedy and attempt to squeeze the last ounce of profit from your speculation.*

To be more specific, my advice—which is Profit-Aid 18—insists: *Always sell a stock when it is within ten percent of its ultimate.*

As emphasized in Chapter 4, all investments should be made as cold, analytical appraisals of ultimate percentage return on investment. This is especially true if you are buying stocks of companies you think will merge, liquidate, or sell out in the near future. When you can foresee large percentage gains with but small loss possibilities, you can relax—but so often in these situations the reverse is true (after the news of merger, liquidation, or sellout is published) and your upside potentials are small in relation to the downside risks.

Simple as this reasoning is, I am amazed at how few people truly understand the vast percentage differences which can and do exist over the life of a merger, liquidation, or sellout "play." Take, for example, the case of the ABC Company, whose stock is now selling at $20 per share. You believe ABC will make a deal of some kind which will make it worth $40 per share. Obviously, a rise from $20 to $40 amounts to a one-hundred-percent gain. Being a shrewd speculator, you also calculate right at the start your downside risks. In the case of ABC you figure that the stock could conceivably decline to, say, $10 per share under poor market conditions or if the event you foresee does not occur. A $20 stock dropping to $10 amounts to a fifty-percent reversal. Thus, right from the start you see your speculation as possessing a potential one-hundred-percent advance *vs.* a possible fifty-percent decline. You should then make your decision based on this and on your calculation of the odds of your contemplated "deal" going through.

Incidentally, let me digress just for a moment. All of this discussion so far sounds like a gambling approach—and I want to spell out unequivocally that playing mergers, et al., is just that: gambling, or, in higher-level terms preferred by the investment business, speculation. Nonetheless, since money can be made from such ventures and since it is inevitable in your investing lifetime that you will come across such decisions, I want to cover the subject.

Now back to our ABC example. You bought ABC at $20 and your timing fortunately proved correct; the stock subsequently rose to $30. Now recalculate your figures, as follows:

$30 stock possibly going to $40 = a 33-percent profit ($10 profit ÷ $30 market price = .33, or 33 percent)
$30 stock possibly dropping to $10 = a 66-percent loss ($20 loss ÷ $30 market price = .66, or 66 percent)

How the percentages have changed! Based on these, you had better feel very sure that your "deal" will be consummated. Otherwise, you stand to lose—from these price levels —twice as much as you stand to gain.

I will never forget the time Honolulu Oil proposed a liquidation of its assets—a liquidation which was to pay out $102.50 per share to its owners. As the payout date approached, Honolulu stock rose steadily and was in the low nineties with about a month to go. I immediately advised people holding the stock to sell it—on the theory expounded above. At first thought, a number of them argued that the seven to ten points left in the stock if held to 102½ was too much money to "throw away." But the percentage approach made sense to them, and most did sell. Interesting to note is the fact the Honolulu stock took two severe nosedives after this; although the patient holder did get his 102½, he had some very unhappy moments the last thirty days. Had the liquidation been blocked (the government attempted vigorously to do so), Honolulu stock could well have sunk to the sixties, which would have amounted to a thirty-to-thirty-five-percent loss from the nineties; when compared with the *maximum* ten-percent-gain potential, it simply didn't make sense.

Naturally, the complete liquidation of a company (such as Honolulu) presents different prospects from, for example, a merger. Most liquidations involve a flat payout in cash and thus there is nothing beyond this payout to consider (actually, the case of Honolulu was not totally in cash, but the securities distributed along with the dollars were all publicly traded already and thus did not involve any "hidden" values). As mentioned, an investor has what should be a simple decision to make in assessing his holding in a to-be-liquidated company; it involves simply a determination of potential gains or losses from current levels—all of which ties in to Profit-Aid 18 about letting the other guy take that last ten percent.

Far more common than liquidation is the merger, and while the general principle of risk *vs.* reward is unchanged, the merger demands further thought on your part. As a matter of fact, it is amazing how many people fail to realize the responsibility of determining (in a merger) what the new *combined* unit may be worth. I stated at the close of our last chapter that "zero plus zero equals zero" in that two poor companies combining will probably add nothing to either. By the same token, one plus one may well total *more than* two when two strong or complementary companies combine. And the person assessing his merger "workout" value must certainly take the new prospects in mind. Your to-be-merged stock may rest within ten percent of its *apparent* value, which should prompt one to get rid of it, but the new unit may have attraction that has not yet been recognized by the investment community. In other words, what looks to be ten-percent ultimate reward may be but a fraction of what really lies ahead.

While there are literally thousands of illustrations which could be used to prove the point, one very vivid one in mind goes back as far as 1958, when the Monroe Calculator Company was in the process of merging into Litton Industries. Monroe on its own had been a steady earner, but its stock had not been a spectacular capital-gain vehicle. As the merger date with Litton moved closer, Monroe stock moved closer and closer to its prescribed value in Litton stock—but this was hardly a case where the shareholder should have acted on our "ten-percent rule." This is because an analysis of the deal led one to a very bullish conclusion for the combined companies; in short, Litton had some exceptional technological capabilities and the move with Monroe was an obvious trend toward setting up a well-rounded business-machine division. In addition, the merger added importantly to Litton's profits per share and it was reasonable to assume that this stock would sell at considerably higher levels after the consolidation, both because of this new earnings level and because the new company would take on a more glamorous rating (perhaps a higher P/E) due to the office-equipment image.

Thus, you can see that a person should carry his merger decision to the next step and find out whether one and one makes two, three, one and a half, four, or what—and you should never take your "ten-percent" step without going through this process. In doing so, always remember that mergers do often break off, and sometimes right at the final moment. But then, this is no more than the "risk" part of your risk-reward thinking process, and the fact still remains that you should let the other fellow take the big gamble for the potential small gain and that you should strive for the large profit while taking minimal risks, wherever possible.

Chapter Nineteen

How and When
to Sell Cyclical Stocks

I imagine you now realize how I feel about investing in companies which have violent ups and downs over the years (companies which are extremely sensitive to the inevitable business cycles and which are typical straight, nongrowth, cyclical issues). I simply prefer to put my money in companies which are *not* sensitive this way, but which instead can be expected to grow steadily through thick and thin.

Nonetheless, I am the first to admit that money can be made from owning cyclical stocks. Basically, the philosophy behind making money from cyclical stocks is very simple: buy them when they are depressed (when their business is poor and investors are selling them because of their discouragement over the bad earnings reports and gloomy near-term prospects) and then sell them when they are in favor again (earning prospects of the companies have changed from very poor to exceptionally good). Although the first part of this philosophy—i.e., buying when conditions are depressed—is hard enough to do, the second essential, of selling when conditions are rosy, is even harder to accomplish temperamentally. It takes objective, clear-thinking, nonemotional, trained minds to come to a sell conclusion when everything looks especially bright. And since we all know that objective, clear-thinking, nonemotional, trained minds always do better than biased, muddled, emotional, *un*trained gray matter, we should do everything possible to equip ourselves to make decisions that the former will make, rather than the latter.

But, you might be wondering, why is it so terribly difficult for people to train themselves to sell these cyclical stocks at the obvious opportune moments when they (the stocks) are *up* in price? Aside from the psychological reasons (i.e., human greed, etc.), there is one important element which lulls people into a (false) sense of security, which in turn forces them to continue holding these stocks instead of disposing of them. *This element,* which, of course, is also responsible for investors buying cyclicals at the wrong times, *is the apparent attraction of an extremely low price-earnings multiple.*

Naturally we all want to buy reasonably priced stocks; thus, we are always on the lookout for—and are attracted by—stocks which are "cheap" on the basis of earnings. But a stock is "cheap" only if its profits continue at present levels or improve therefrom. In the case of cyclical stocks, you can be sure that profits will come tumbling down at some not-too-distant date. Thus, the low P/E, which is computed on the basis of temporary, inflated earnings, is not a true P/E at all. For example, consider the case of the ABC Machinery Company. Here is its record of earnings over the last ten years:

Year	Earnings per Share
1966	$4.00
1965	2.00
1964	3.00
1963	1.00
1962	4.00
1961	1.00
1960	2.00
1959	Loss 1.00
1958	2.00
1957	4.00

ABC's past record is the typical up-and-down, erratic pattern of a highly cyclical company: a boom year in 1957 followed by lower results in 1958 and a loss in 1959; a fair year in 1960, lower again in 1961, way up in 1962, way down in 1963, favorable in 1964, slightly lower in 1965, and booming again in 1966. With this kind of history in mind, is it reasonable to view 1966's performance as "normal"? Absolutely not! Then why should you expect a "normal P/E" for the stock? The answer is: you should *not!*

Despite this reasonable thinking, there are always investors who lose sight of the facts and become completely enamored with the low P/E. For example, there are those who would consider ABC stock cheap at $40 per share "because it is selling for only ten times 1966's earnings of $4.00 per share." This is their only argument, and it is one which is made without any real study or thought. Actually, this is the point where ABC stock should be *sold*, not bought. This conclusion is based on the following thinking, which really tears holes in their argument:

1. A study of ABC's history proves it is going to be an erratic earner.
2. The year 1966 looks like one of the occasional peak years.
3. The odds are strong that either 1967 or 1968 will show a sharp reversal *downward* in profits.
4. ABC's *average annual earnings* over the past four years has been *$2.50 per share* ($4.00 + 2.00 + 3.00 + 1.00 = $10.00 ÷ 4 years = $2.50 per-share average).
5. ABC stock at $40 per share is selling at sixteen times the $2.50-per-share average.
6. When ABC is back earning only $2.00 per share again (which it will undoubtedly be at some time in the very near future), *the stock at $40 will be twenty times earnings.*

Thus, a stock which appeared cheap to the casual observer becomes overpriced upon objective thinking.

Naturally, our thinking on ABC would include an appraisal of both industry and company conditions to determine whether anything has occurred which would alter its up-and-down, no-growth-trend pattern. In the vast majority of cases in viewing cyclical companies, however, you will find that there is no basic change and that the historical pattern will give you a clue of what to expect in the future.

It is this kind of approach which would have kept people away from steels, railroads, and other typical cyclical-industry groups on a long-term basis. And it is this kind of thinking which especially would have kept people from buying such stocks at the top of their cycle. Indeed, it is this approach which should prompt people to sell these stocks near their highs.

At any rate, an important lesson is to be remembered here, and it is to be summarized as our Profit-Aid 19, as follows:

1. *Never figure a cyclical company's attractiveness on the basis of boom earnings.*
2. *Understand that such a typical nongrowth cyclical does not deserve a normal multiple.*
3. *Utilize average earnings over the past three to four years as the basis for the "correct" P/E.*
4. *Always figure what the P/E might be when the cycle changes and profits are depressed once again.*

Utilization of this Profit-Aid provides you with a strong defense against some common mistakes made in stocks, and it likewise gives you the proper perspective to take the offensive (make-money) approach to cyclical-type investments.

Chapter Twenty

Investing in the "Fourth Stringers"

There are really two basic methods of investing in the stock market. You can invest in the proven companies and feel confident that a continuation of their success in the future will provide you with gains. Or you can invest in the lesser-known, not-so-proven companies, hoping they will have greater success in the future than they have thus far achieved. In the first instance, you are investing in the present "first stringers"; in the second case, you are putting your money in second, third, and fourth stringers—hoping they will someday make the first string.

I am not going to debate the merits of these two approaches here. You know, of course, that the first stringers are usually more secure and far more reliable but that you can make a lot more money if you pick out a fourth stringer which suddenly jumps ahead and is recognized as a first rater.

When you are analyzing businesses, however, it is seldom you find a company which is on top of the heap in all its areas. This would be asking a great deal. General Electric is a good example. GE is well diversified (all products fit a pattern) and is a leader in countless fields. But it is not necessarily *the* leader in everything it tackles. And this fact is certainly not a sign of weakness. Yet there are companies which are not tops in anything and which are well behind their competitors straight across the board. Here is where you as an investor have to be careful—and this is the reason for this chapter.

First of all, let's picture what it is to be a "straggler" in this competitive business world. You are always fighting an uphill battle: your products usually lack the blind acceptance you like to have; you have to spend more money on advertising just to retain your not-so-rosy position; you are not the price-setter in your field; and you have a harder time attracting proper management talent. Take a company like Allis Chalmers. Whereas a decade ago Allis Chalmers stock was fairly well regarded in investment circles, I was extremely negative on its outlook. Why? Mainly because I saw it as a consistent third and fourth stringer in *all* its lines of endeavor. It was always well behind GE and Westinghouse in the business of producing electric generators; it was always behind Deere and Caterpillar in the heavy-construction-equipment field. Unless you could see something entirely new developing at Allis Chalmers I could never understand people buying its stock for growth. Time certainly bore out this reasoning, as Allis Chalmers was one of the truly disappointing stocks of the 1950–1966 era. I tell you this merely to illustrate this all-important point. Had this company had one or two major areas in which it had some kind of commanding position, it might have been able to overcome the negative investment result.

While Radio Corporation of America cannot be considered as a third rater, I suspect that the company's inability to become the very best in its important areas of concentration (prior to the advent of color TV, that is) was partly responsible for its stock being a very mediocre performer over the post-World War II period. All in all, I think it had generally been accepted that:

Zenith was a more successful TV manufacturer.
Lockheed was a better military contractor.
CBS was a more successful telecaster.
IBM was a far superior data processor.

Thus, you can see that I do not subscribe to the theory that size alone is any criterion for attractiveness. As a matter of fact, size without some real dominance can be a great disadvantage.

For this reason, I suggest you conduct your own "dominance" rating of a company you are considering for investment. This rating procedure, which is Profit-Aid 20, involves two bits of advice, namely:

1. *Take an objective look at a company's product lines and determine whether it has a commanding or semi-commanding position anywhere.*
2. *Determine in how many areas it is swimming upstream and is in a poor competitive position.*

This kind of analysis will prove very helpful in giving you the right "feel" about the company and its prospects.

Success in Something Small vs. *Mere Existence in Something Big!*

I think most people will agree with the old adage that it can be more satisfying to be a large frog in a small pond than a small frog in a large pond. This is true when investing, too. I would much prefer to invest in a company which has, or promises to have, success in a small field than put my money into an outfit which is all over the map but which is not particularly successful anywhere. A good illustration of this involves my discovery of Masco Corporation, a stock which proved extremely rewarding to my clients—appreciating in value about ten times in less than two years and about twenty-five times over a six-year span. Masco's major business was the manufacture of its Delta one-lever faucet (which had a patented feature of only one moving part). Now, ordinarily I wouldn't invest a penny in the plumbing industry; in fact, I had absolutely no interest (just a negative feeling) about those companies which were engaged in this usually unexciting, highly competitive field. It so happens, however, that the one-lever faucet was one of the fastest-growing segments of this industry, and Masco's product, combined with strong marketing, gave it what appeared to me to be an exciting potential. The company had a specialty item and was able to put all its efforts into making this product a great success. This gave it a great advantage over its competition—all of which had to be concerned with bathtubs, basins, water closets, and hundreds of other items.

Another vivid illustration exists in the liquor business. It is interesting to note that among the least successful stocks in this field in recent years have been two very large participants, Schenley Industries and National Distillers—while specialty companies such as Paddington (J & B Scotch), James Beam Distilling (Jim Beam), and Brown-Forman (Jack Daniel's a large contributor) did quite well. The smaller companies were able to concentrate on their very profitable lines and were not burdened with the huge inventories and marketing headaches which the large producers had in their across-the-board lines.

There are many other examples like Masco and the liquor companies, giving proof to the fact that it is better to invest in a successful specialty company than in a relatively unsuccessful large company which covers all aspects of its business but which lacks the control over profitability that it would like to enjoy.

Conclusion

You can see from this discussion just how flexible your thinking has to be in the stock market. You want to buy first stringers, even if they are first string in only a segment of the overall business. Businessmen nowadays are learning that sales volume is not the important criterion of success. It is, instead, *profits* which signify management efficiency, and so many times the specialty company—the big frog in the small pond—produces the best results.

Chapter Twenty-one

How to Avoid Fad Investments

In the lineup of dos and don'ts in the stock market, one of the important points is *not* to invest in fad industries or fad stocks. In short, avoid fads of all kinds.

This is equally good advice for businessmen—who are just as subject to fads in their future planning as the general public is when it comes to investing. Now, maybe you think I am referring only to small businessmen—the kind who get into hula-hoop manufacture and the trampoline business right at the end of their fad cycles. But this is not my contention. Even very large corporations, which have the benefits of market research and other experts in their planning, too often become sheep and follow the ideas of others blindly. When they do, they get into trouble (just like the hula-hoop and trampoline latecomers), and their stockholders suffer accordingly.

History has shown that whenever one field or one product area becomes glamorous, many otherwise rational businessmen cannot resist the urge to join the flock. I guess the sociologists would tell us it's strictly a matter of human group behavior; and the psychologists would say that it is typical of the human mind. Human nature hasn't changed much over the last thousand years, and the urge to follow others is completely normal. Just as an individual finds it difficult to stand by while his friends and associates are buying a certain style clothing, most corporate management finds it very hard to see its competition expanding into certain directions without feeling the impulse to do the same. Just as the completely independent individual is an exception, the businessman who can stand alone and resist the temptation to join his competition in some mad rush is likewise an unusual character.

The reason I am dwelling on this subject is that its full understanding can save you countless dollars in the stock market. In the course of your investment life you will encounter many, many cases in which certain companies rush to join the herd in some new and apparently glamorous pursuits. Your natural inclination will be to invest in these pursuits, and I want you to know what your odds for success are before you start.

It is obvious from the definition of the word "fad" (a *passing* fashion, craze, or hobby) that anything qualifying under that label should be avoided. But my discussion goes a lot deeper than this. Many suddenly popular areas are not passing fashions at all. They may be completely basic and essential. But a strong warning is necessary here, too. You see, massive competition from new entries into a field invariably leads to a weakening of the price structure of the industry— and this generally means lower profits for all concerned, at least temporarily.

For illustration, think back over the past decade. Consider what has happened in some of the areas which became almost universally accepted as "products of the future."

Which come to your mind?

Aluminum?

Transistors?

Plastics?

Synthetic fibers?

Boating, bowling, and other leisure-time "products"?

Computers?

All "fantastic growth areas of the future." And what happened in these fields? Well, let's see.

In aluminum, the Big Four (Aluminium, Alcoa, Kaiser, and Reynolds) were expanding as though demand would never stop growing. Then Anaconda and Olin Mathieson decided to build large facilities and get in on the "gravy train." When their plants came on-stream, the supply-demand condition in the industry was altered considerably and the price structure broke down, thereby creating problems and lower profits for all.

Few industries captured the imagination of businessmen and investors alike as the semiconductor field, headed by the glamorous little device which was replacing the vacuum tube —the transistor. One company, Texas Instruments, had carved out a healthy beginning from the manufacture of transistors. Market studies showed how many billions of these little items would be needed in the near future, and suddenly countless companies, in both related and unrelated fields of endeavor, decided to hop aboard. Fairchild Camera, Motorola, General Transistor; then Clevite, Rheem Manufacturing, Universal Controls, and many others. The result is now history. Transistor prices came down sharply, the enlarged capacity divided the business among many firms—all of which meant reduced sales and sharply lower income (and, in the case of most of the new entrants, large losses).

The chemical business has also been notorious for such overexpansion. Which is just what occurred in the synthetic-fiber and plastics areas, despite the fact that there was anything but a diminishing demand for these products. Synthetic fiber was a magic word at one time. Then, after Du Pont's basic patent on nylon ran out, such giants as American Cyanamid, Eastman Kodak, Monsanto, and American Viscose moved in. While this is no story of disaster, a series of price cuts developed, and most of the new participants had rough sledding at the beginning.

Experiences in polyethylene were similar. The word "polyethylene" had become a glamour symbol, that is, before a host of oil companies and chemical outfits entered the scene. After that, it became standard procedure to read in annual reports and other company statements about the unfortunate experiences in polyethylene. Most managements labeled these experiences in terms such as "unforeseen competitive conditions" and "unfortunate price reductions which took place," etc. But, to the student of basic business and basic human nature, these should not have been unforeseen at all, and the fact that unfortunate price reductions took place should have been expected.

The boating industry was another example, although in all due fairness, this reeked of fad—and pure fad. Nonetheless, the fact remains that a whole host of new manufacturers entered this limited field, and the result was catastrophic for most. Bowling alleys, already discussed, followed this very trend.

Lastly, for the sake of this discussion, the computer field was one which had unbelievable glamour and which promised dramatic growth in the years ahead. Yet the combined entries of Honeywell, General Electric, Radio Corporation of America, National Cash Register, Burroughs, Sperry Rand, and countless others, along with the leader, IBM, were just too much. As late as 1966, there were but a few companies in the United States which admitted to making a profit in computers.

It seems that every year or two some new field generates the irresistible enthusiasm which attracts a host of entrants. It is my analysis, for example, that the glamorous electronics field will follow the same pattern: glamour, attraction, mass entry, competition, price weakness, and, finally, lack of profitability. (This is very much of a fragmented industry, however, and results will vary widely from segment to segment.)

So you can see the dangers of investing in companies which are already in or which are suddenly entering a soon-to-be-crowded area. No matter how bright the outlook may be for the products involved, the mere fact that there has been a massive entry makes it very vulnerable.

Profit-Aid 21, which follows, is designed to give you a better understanding of how both businesses and stock buyers react to plain old human nature and create almost identical cycles for themselves. Your understanding of these inevitable cycles should keep you from falling into their traps—and will teach you how, instead, to profit from them.

I urge you to read over the following illustration very carefully. It depicts a pattern typical of so many industries. The writing on top of the lines indicates the conditions within the industry itself, and the comments below the line reflect what the stock market is generally doing at the same moment.

If you think about the industries discussed earlier, you will note that each followed a cycle such as this—and the stocks of many major companies within each industry followed the identical pattern shown. Of course, this means that stock buyers were generally "zigging" when they should have been "zagging" and vice versa—but, then, that is just what the public normally does. The obvious buy points exist at 1 and 4, whereas the masses were probably just taking their initial positions at the latter stages of 2 and 6. Equally important in this Profit-Aid is the realization that maximum profits are made through selling at these 2 and 6 levels. In other words, industries going through stages such as this are not normally "stick-away-forever" investments (computers may prove to be an exception).

On the same subject, a person should be extremely cautious of enthusiasm which will crop up for industries which have lacked consistent patterns in the past. It is one thing to buy an unappreciated stock or industry when it is available at a price which reflects this lack of understanding (at a low price-earnings multiple; at points 1 and 4). It is another thing to buy same after it has become universally popular and is commanding a premium P/E (points 2 and 6). In the latter case, you are probably following a fad, particularly if the company or industry involved has never exhibited much consistency in sales and earnings progress in the past.

The purpose of all this is to protect you against what so many have suffered for over the years in the market. We all

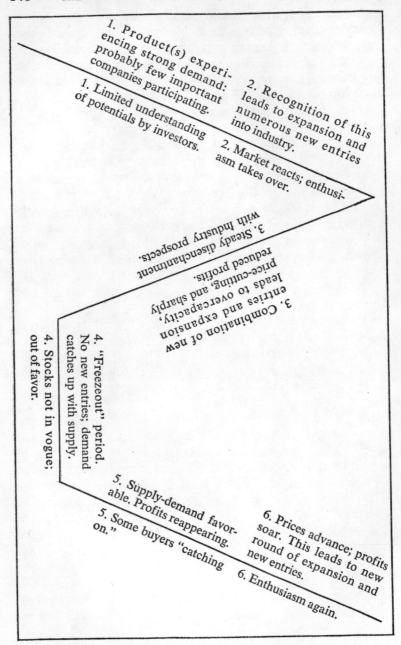

1. Product(s) experiencing strong demand: probably few important companies participating.

1. Limited understanding of potentials by investors.

2. Recognition of this leads to expansion and numerous new entries into industry.

2. Market reacts; enthusiasm takes over.

3. Steady disenchantment with industry prospects.

3. Combination of new entries and expansion leads to overcapacity, price-cutting, and sharply reduced profits.

4. "Freezeout" period. No new entries; demand catches up with supply.

4. Stocks not in vogue; out of favor.

5. Supply-demand favorable. Profits reappearing.

5. Some buyers "catching on."

6. Prices advance; profits soar. This leads to new round of expansion and new entries.

6. Enthusiasm again.

know that it is always better to be the shepherd than to be the sheep; and I do not want you to become sheep in your investments, because if you do, you will only end up where all the sheep do—either shorn or slaughtered.

The understanding of Profit-Aid 21 should provide you with the sophistication which will protect you against falling into inevitable cycle traps. Indeed, it should enable you to profit from same!

Chapter Twenty-two

Realizing When the Odds
Are Stacked Against You

I have heard it kiddingly said many times that an expert is "anyone from out of town." For some reason human beings seem to think that an out-of-town specialist on a subject is often more authoritative than even the most astute local personalities. Perhaps this is because there is an aura of mystery about a person from another region; perhaps it is because we are introduced to him for his attributes (without knowing his mistakes or failures); or perhaps it is all merely an extension of the axiom "the grass is always greener on the other side of the street."

There is a limit, however, to this thesis on expertise. I *can* understand it when it comes to a subject which is common and the same to all areas—but it certainly does *not* hold water about a local subject. For example, I can appreciate an out-of-towner having the respect of a New York audience on a general subject such as "Achieving Proper City Lighting" or "The Economic Outlook for the United States"—but it would be difficult to accept as expert a non-New Yorker on a spe-

150

cific such as "Dressing for the Climate in New York" or "Where to Dine in New York."

The reason I have gone to the trouble of this explanation is that, as you have no doubt guessed, it has a parallel to our subject—the stock market. The fact is that some investors in the market never seem to learn the lesson that they are bucking significant odds in trying to mastermind situations which are completely detached from them.

One excellent illustration of this detached ineptness is demonstrated by the gyrations which took place in 1964 in the common stock of Fifth Avenue Coach Lines, Inc., New York City's bus line. The line had been seized by the city, and stockholders were to be compensated based on the decision of the State Supreme Court (a condemnation judgment was to place a value on the properties taken over). Quite a disparity existed between what the company claimed its assets to be worth and the evaluation of the city and its Board of Estimate. Fifth Avenue had asked to be paid the huge sum of $112,523,-000, whereas the city had appraised the properties at a maximum of $24,000,000. After allowing for company liabilities outstanding (and omitting certain other increments which might have been forthcoming to shareholders), the first figure would have produced around $116.50 per share for Fifth Avenue stockholders, while the latter figure meant a paltry $7.00.

To speculate on the outcome of this forced liquidation, I would certainly feel the necessity of having some kind of "inside track"; if I did not have this, my judgment would tell me to avoid the situation entirely. To do otherwise would constitute out-and-out gambling!

Needless to say, many never considered this kind of advice, as proved by the fact that Fifth Avenue stock rose from a low of $11 in early 1964 to as high as $37 later in the year—prior to the decision rendered by the court.

When the announcement came—that the "fair value" as fixed by the court amounted to slightly over thirty million dollars—Fifth Avenue stock plummeted 14⅜ points in one day (from 32⅞ on Friday, August 14, to 18½ on the following Monday). But this is not the full lesson at all. A personal experience took place on that Monday which serves as an excellent illustration of the point in mind, one which should delineate some more common sense investment philosophy.

On that fateful (to some) Monday, a valued friend and client of mine called me on the phone. Great excitement was in his tone of voice. He had seen the precipitous drop take place in Fifth Avenue stock (at the time of his call, the stock was actually around $15 per share) and he was naturally attracted because of it. He knew the wisdom of doing the opposite of what emotional people do in the buying and selling of securities. In addition, he had read an article which appeared that morning in *The Wall Street Journal* regarding the whole Fifth Avenue development. This article stated that the company would receive more than the value of the award from the courts; most analysts, according to the *WSJ*, placed the value "between $15 and $17.50 a share."

At any rate, this individual was ready and willing to take a position in Fifth Avenue stock based on the combination of the accentuated weakness and the potential liquidating value, which could conceivably have proved higher than the figure discussed in the newspaper article.

Fortunately, he sought someone else's judgment, too. He asked me my opinion of his thesis and idea, and my answer was typical, not of any brilliance, but of how common sense can prove rewarding when it comes to the buying and selling of stocks. My answer was simply:

"Look, _____, think of the huge volume of trading which is now taking place in Fifth Avenue Coach stock. No doubt, many hundreds of people are involved in the decisions which are taking place. Here you are—one person with no 'inside' knowledge—and you are some three thousand miles away from the 'information center' on this security. You are basing your hopes on a newspaper article and, by doing so, are just one of the masses."

In essence, I was simply saying that other people were in a far better position to know the real facts than my friend was.

As mentioned, this deduction took no real intelligence—just a practical approach. Some simple logic and common sense was enough to shake my friend into a realization that the odds were stacked against him from the start in either the buying or the selling of Fifth Avenue stock.

As it turned out, it was fortunate that we took no action on this day. Over the next nine months, Fifth Avenue declined from the $15 figure (the price at which it was trading when he telephoned) to around $8.50.

As stated, any strategist knows that both offense and defense are required in arriving at a rounded attack. I hope the above adds one more defensive "trick" to your arsenal of stock-market knowledge. Profit-Aid 22, therefore, is but an extension of the adage about the shoemaker sticking to his last; in our case, it becomes: *When dealing with stocks in which specific information is the criterion for purchase, avoid completely those in which you are, in reality, detached.*

Chapter Twenty-three

Refuting Some
"Sure-Fire" Success Theories

A. INVESTING IN THE "CHOSEN LOT"

Many investors feel secure having their money in only the country's most widely held stocks. Whether they get a feeling of security knowing that they have a lot of company in their investments or whether they simply believe it is safer and smarter being with the crowd, there exists just such a cult who only want the "chosen lot." Naturally, there are arguments for this kind of thinking. The most important argument is that the widely held stocks are the large companies, the substantial companies, the corporate giants—and how can you go wrong investing in these? As I will repeat over and over in this book, however, size alone is no guarantee of success, and thus choice by size surely does not ensure investment rewards. Blind choice without independent judgment and analysis is indeed a dangerous approach.

As a matter of fact, there are some strong arguments which should convince you that the chosen lot is not at all a paved road to the pot of gold. First of all, the fact that a stock is widely held indicates that there is broad public ownership. But is this good? Not necessarily! As you have no doubt already learned, the public is generally *wrong*. Thus, by doing

154

some geometric thinking you might come up with the following corollary: that investing in the most widely held issues is investing in what the public likes, which in turn means that the chances for great success are slim.

Secondly, the stocks which boast the greatest number of shareholders are usually those which have many millions of shares outstanding. Needless to say, the companies with huge numbers of shares outstanding ("large capitalizations," as we say in the investment business) need large new developments to keep their growth alive. Whereas a small company might require only one or two new products or developments to bring about large increases in sales and earnings, the company of large size needs many such additions—which it may or may not be able to produce consistently. By the same token, many large companies get bogged down with paperwork, organization charts, limited chance for rapid advancement for workers, etc. Or they may get so large they may become subject to governmental interference. These latter negatives may or may not take place, but at least the risks are worth pointing out.

Thirdly, the fact that a stock is widely held poses one more risk: that the shareholders may change their opinion of the stock's prospects and start a massive liquidation. The fact that many, many shares would suddenly appear for sale on the market means that many, many buyers would have to be found, lest the stock not drop sharply in price.

Just in case you think I am being only theoretical about this discussion, I would like to forward some concrete examples for your consideration. In 1961 I came across an old publication which listed the nation's most widely held securities of a few years before. In glancing down this list, I was interested to see how the stocks had fared in the market in the ensuing few years. The results were disappointing, to say the least. So you, too, can see how these stocks progressed, I decided to divide them into the following categories:

Those stocks which performed extremely well.
Those stocks which performed well.
Those stocks which did only fair.
Those stocks which performed poorly.

Extremely Well	Well	Fair	Poor
None	American Telephone	General Motors	Standard Oil of N.J.
	Columbia Gas	General Electric	U.S. Steel
	Standard Oil of Calif.	Ford	Socony Mobil
	Consolidated Edison	Du Pont	Bethlehem Steel
	Sears Roebuck	Radio Corp. of America	Sperry Rand
	Commonwealth Edison		Standard Oil of Indiana
	Texaco		Cities Service
			Westinghouse

Out of the twenty stocks, none did extremely well, seven did well, five did fair, and eight did poorly. Six years later, in 1967, I made a new assessment—and my scoreboard looked like this:

Extremely Well	Well	Fair	Poor
None	Texaco	Sears Roebuck	American Telephone
	Radio Corp. of America	General Motors	Columbia Gas
	Socony Mobil	General Electric	Commonwealth Edison
	Standard Oil of Indiana	Sperry Rand	Consolidated Edison
	Westinghouse	Cities Service	Du Pont
		Ford	U.S. Steel
			Bethlehem Steel
			Standard Oil of Calif.
			Standard Oil of N.J.

Once again, performance left much to be desired. Before you jump to some incorrect conclusions, let me emphasize that it is not my intent to discourage people from owning large, widely held corporations per se. I subscribe to the theory that select blue-chip issues constitute the most assured road to success and that they should form the foundation of one's portfolio. But we must be frank and say that "huddling together" with the masses is not the answer.

Some of the broadly held stocks are going to be good ones, but the fact that a multitude of shareholders exists should not become your criterion in choosing stocks. Investors should concentrate on quality in their investments, but bigness and breadth of ownership by themselves do not signify quality.

Before closing this subject, let me pass on a summary of all this, plus one important additional tip, all of which I am lumping into Profit-Aid 23: *Be extremely cautious about the ownership of too many of the top twenty most widely held stocks, and be especially wary of new entries into this or other broad-ownership classes.*

Apropos of the latter (new entries), every so often a "strange name" will creep into the limelight. It may suddenly appear in the list of widely held stocks or it may pop up as a favorite of MIP (Monthly Investment Plan—New York Stock Exchange) buyers.

Consider the case of the "riches-to-rags" bowling twins previously discussed (American Machine & Foundry and Brunswick). Without analyzing the pros and cons of these two companies, it could hardly have been debatable that they possessed the stature or investment caliber of an IBM or Eastman Kodak. In short, both had to be classified as "businessman's-risk" equities as opposed to blue-chip, growth-without-interruption stocks.

With this in mind, it might have (I should say "should have") startled wise investors to learn that both suddenly vaulted into the MIP Fifty Most Popular Stocks list in the year 1961. Almost from nowhere, the date of November 24, 1961, found Brunswick as number 35 and AMF as number 43.

Now, some people might have interpreted this "rise to stardom" as a strong plus factor for both stocks. I would *not!* Quite the contrary! One of the important points of all this

discussion revolves around the *kind* of purchasing support
stocks receive. And my focus on widely held (or MIP) equities is another way of assessing what might be termed *weak
ownership*. In short, buying by a lot of investors fails to im-
press me and, as a matter of fact, only points to this type of
weaker, less-sophisticated, less-informed purchasing.

It is important to realize that what happened to the bowling babies was hardly an isolated example. To prove the
point, I went over the MIP favorites for each year since
1960. With but a few exceptions, the appearance of new
names could be crudely termed "the kiss of death." In 1962,
for example, Scott Paper and Ford Motor made the favorite
list for the first time—and five years later neither had produced a profit for their owners. The next year did find Xerox
aboard, but all three of the other entries (Corn Products,
General Foods, and Lone Star Gas) were losers as of this writing (1967). In 1964 there was a host of strange names, including International Harvester, City Products, Johnson &
Johnson, American Bakeries, Florida Power, Worthington,
Rexall, and Lucky Stores. Hindsight reveals that only a few
performed admirably if held until now. The next year
(1965) found Comsat, Transamerica, Chrysler, Honeywell,
Control Data, and Chesebrough-Pond's as new entries; at
least there was improvement here, as the final two names experienced good results. Just for the record, new MIP's as of
mid-December, 1966, were Caterpillar Tractor, American
Hospital Supply, FMC Corp., Polaroid, Pan American World
Airways, and Baxter Laboratories.

Just as revealing were many stocks which dropped from
the Favorite Fifty over the years. In most cases they apparently had become less popular just when they should have
been bought heavily. Such successful investments as American Airlines, Polaroid, Pepsico, Socony Mobil, and Texas Instruments were omitted at times when they were in reality
most attractively priced.

At any rate, the record speaks for itself: overall, the
"chosen lot" has not been so well chosen. Thus, the theory
advanced by others needs refutation; and, most important, a
study of the facts provides us with another method of com-

mon sense stock selection. One of the most reliable sell signals might well be the use of contrary thinking about widely held and, most particularly, "bought-by-smaller-investors" favorites.

B. FOLLOWING THE MUTUAL FUNDS

Another theory advanced by many to achieve success in the stock market involves following the investment trusts (mutual funds, closed-end investment companies). On casual observation this theory sounds valid; after all, these institutions employ many analysts and, as a whole, they certainly qualify as experts. In this age of specialization, the trained expert should outperform the untrained, and thus the person who parallels the moves made by these large institutions has a greatly improved chance for success. Or does he?

I say he really does not!

But why? Why doesn't this apparently logical theory hold water as a sure-fire road to success in the market?

To my way of thinking, there are numerous reasons for not adhering to his philosophy, as follows:

1. *Analyzing the actions of the funds is downright confusing.* I advise you sometime to analyze the quarterly reports of the many investment trusts. In the vast majority of cases, you will find that what one investment company is selling, another is buying. So you will find yourself confronted with this kind of confusion: You will ponder what to do when, for example, Lehman Corp. and Eaton and Howard are buyers of a given security and Tri-Continental, Affiliated, and Massachusetts Investors are selling it. Your answer to this might be to choose one or two investment companies which are outperforming the others and follow these only. The only trouble here is that most of these companies go in spurts. Lazard and Lehman, for example, might be outdistancing their rivals when the oil stocks as a group are in favor and are moving, because these two trusts have always specialized in the petroleum areas and have

possibly larger holdings in this field than other trusts. MIT Growth Stock Fund and Diversified Growth will shine best when the high P/E growth issues are in vogue. And so forth! Or you might find a great preponderance of selling by the trusts in a stock, but you might think highly of the one trust which is, at the time, buying this issue. All in all, it is safe to say that it is difficult to come to a definite conclusion from the actions of the funds alone, and I would rather leave my mind clear and unmuddled and concentrate on the important considerations which I hope have been made clear in this book.

2. *Investment companies are anything but infallible.* No one, of course, is always right—whether you are talking about life's general problems or the stock market. But some people expect close to perfection from their investment advisors and some actually believe that the investment experts, with all their wisdom and "inside information," are not going to make fatal mistakes. Unfortunately this is not true. The fact is that the investment companies are not machines. They are made up of human beings. And, being human, they are subject to some of the emotional mistakes that individuals make. In short, they can be wrong, too, and thus your following their actions blindly is not like following an instructor in mathematics, in which your conformance will lead you to the right answer one hundred percent of the time.

3. *You learn about trust investment decisions after they have had an effect on the market.* More important than number 2 above is the realization that you learn what stocks the trusts have bought and sold *after* they have done so, not before. This is important, because large purchases or sales can change market prices significantly. This is especially true of the large investment trusts. When Trust A decides to accumulate one hundred thousand shares of XYZ stock, it does so as deftly as possible, but the overall result will normally be to raise the price of the stock itself. Most trusts operate on

an average-cost policy, wherein they purchase the stock on a consistent basis; they buy as much as possible at the prevailing price but are generally willing to step up to higher prices as time goes on to accumulate what they want. Thus, if they start out buying XYZ at $10 and buy a considerable amount there, they can afford to go up to $11 or $12 or $13 because—when combined with their original purchases of $10—they still end up with a low average cost. The trouble is that you, as a follower, learn about the XYZ acquisition when it is at $13. Percentage returns are all-important and there is quite a difference between owning XYZ at an average cost of $10.50 per share and owning it at $13.

Whether the trust is right or wrong in its investment reasoning, you don't like to buy a stock when it is "artificially" inflated due to one large purchase order.

Naturally, the same thing goes for a stock which has been liquidated by a trust in large proportions. The constant pressure from a one-hundred-thousand-share sell order in the market can drive a stock down sharply. And, of course, you hear about this sale after it has taken place and after the price is so altered.

All of this reasoning is especially valid today—what with many mutual funds actually trading-oriented. Some funds are in and out of stocks so fast that you may be doing just the opposite of what the funds you are "following" are doing at the moment.

4. *The investment trusts are widely diversified and your selection may be isolated.* The idea behind portfolio management is to achieve a very high batting average. Realistically, every manager has to expect some mistakes, but it is hoped these can be overcome by the large percentage of gainers. You may not be able to afford the same kind of diversification and thus your choice may turn out to be one of a small number of "strikeouts." Thus, this lack of success may loom large in your overall picture, whereas it may become buried in their overall scene.

5. *Certain sales by investment companies may be prompted*

by other than investment reasons. Investment companies, as mentioned, want to show results to their stockholders and to the public who constitute potential buyers for their shares. One way of showing investment performance is to distribute large dividends to their stockholders. The regular investment income which is distributed quarterly to stockholders cannot be varied according to the trust's wishes: this payout will depend on all the dividends received from the stocks held in the trust, and these dividends are beyond the control of the trust. In addition to the investment income, however, investment companies distribute the capital gains they have taken during the year. This can vary according to the investment-company policies, and here is where motivation for selling a security can be other than a strict investment opinion. Assume, for example, that Trust A owns some IBM, for which it paid much lower prices a number of years ago. Assume also that this particular year has not been a good one in the general stock market and that Trust A has not sold many stocks at a gain. But Trust A has made it a practice of declaring enough capital gains each year so that its shareholders receive total dividends (investment income plus capital-gains distribution) to bring about a six-percent yield on the present price of Trust A stock. One way this six-percent objective can be achieved this year is to sell off a low-cost stock such as IBM. Trust A management may have little choice if it wants to continue its established policy: it may have to divorce its investment thinking from its desire to create a certain cash return for its shareholders. And thus it might sell IBM or similar stock. You as a follower of investment-company buys and sells could be misled by this; you think that Trust A is discouraged about the prospects for IBM, whereas —as I pointed out—the decision might have been prompted mainly by another consideration.

I do not mean to sound skeptical of investment companies in this discussion. As a matter of fact, I firmly believe in ownership of certain investment trusts. But I do have to be objective and tell you certain internal facts which make the blind following of trust buys and sells a difficult and unsound theory. As they say, there are many ways to skin a cat, and I just want to take some of the air out of this theory—which appears so logical and is so strongly believed by certain investors. When you come right down to it, I suppose it really makes more sense for the person wanting to follow the investment companies to forget about making isolated decisions based on their reported buys and sells and, instead, to have their whole package and own them directly.

C. PORTFOLIO FAVORITES—HELP OR HINDRANCE?

Just as some investors derive a feeling of security from knowing their stocks are widely held by the public, some are inclined to rest easier knowing that the industry groups and/ or individual stocks they own are held in huge proportions in the large portfolios of mutual funds, insurance companies, and other institutions. Just as I proved that the public favorites are not necessarily the ones to own, I have to point out that the institutional choices give no guarantee of success. As a matter of fact, the mere existence in large chunks can (although it is the exception) present a real problem.

Suppose, for example, there is a change of thinking about a given stock or industry group. Not necessarily an extremely negative attitude, but enough change in thinking to warrant a cutback in ownership. Such altered attitude can lead to substantial liquidation by the large holders. You see, it is one thing to have only a small portion of your assets in one field or one company; in this case, you can have a change of thinking and, as long as it is not a strong negative, the owner can easily rationalize the situation and retain his position. The reaction may be to glide over the new look on the horizon and figure the risk is small in holding on—because of the position being small. But it is another and entirely different reaction when a sizable number of eggs are in the basket which suddenly looks not quite as strong as before. In this case, the normal—and prudent—decision is to reduce the holdings and to do it posthaste.

Witness the case of the oil stocks in the mid-1950's. At that time, oils constituted twenty to twenty-five percent of most managed, diversified portfolios—and most investors felt confident about buying the oils because of this concentration and "smart-money" representation. What people failed to consider were the consequences of just a slight change in thinking about this group. Who wants twenty to twenty-five percent of his money tied up in a field with uncertainty? Obviously, such a turnabout in approach would bring a mammoth amount of stock for sale in the market. And this is just what occurred with the oils! A tremendous supply of oil stocks was liquidated—just to bring portfolios down to the point where they were no longer overloaded in this field. A reduction of ten percent in the countless large portfolios, representing many billions of dollars in value, constituted a huge number of shares, and this constant liquidation forced the oils down in price and kept them under pressure for *years* thereafter.

The steel stocks a few years later fell into the same kind of pressure. In this case, the group generally accounted for five to ten percent of the average portfolio, but this is a representative amount—enough to cause sizable selling when doubts about the industry crept into people's minds.

You can see, therefore, that there is not always strength in numbers and that, as a matter of fact, existence in large amounts can be a definite detriment. When there is such a supply to contend with, you need a multitude of buyers to "sop up" the stock offered for sale. In the great percentage of cases, such a multitude hardly exists at one time, and you naturally experience considerable price weakness from the selling.

So now to some practical application of this thesis. Just which groups are held in large percentages by today's institutional investors?

Unfortunately, there is no one compilation of stock holdings for all institutions, including pension funds, endowment funds, insurance companies, investment trusts, etc. We can get a good clue, however, from the figures supplied by the

Investment Company Institute, listing portfolio diversification of the mutual funds in this country as of December 31, 1966. Total assets of these funds were over thirty-five billion dollars on that date, so we are certainly talking about significant holdings. To lend as much accuracy as possible, I have "editorialized" and assessed how the inclusion of other institutions might alter the percentages. Therefore, I have indicated in the right-hand column in the following table those industries which would, in my assessment, have a greater percentage holding with the inclusion of other institutions and those which would probably show smaller representation.

Here is this industry breakdown, which qualifies as Profit-Aid 24:

MUTUAL FUNDS' PORTFOLIO DIVERSIFICATION
PERCENT OF TOTAL COMMON STOCK BY INDUSTRIES
1956–1961–1966

				Estimated Changes, Including Other Institutions	
	1956	1961	1966	Higher	Lower
Agricultural Equipment	0.66%	0.42%	0.77%		
Aircraft Mfg. & Aerospace	2.56	1.26	2.90		x
Air Transport	0.46	0.41	4.72		x
Auto & Accessories (excl. Tires)	2.76	3.51	2.93	x	
Building Materials & Equip.	3.86	2.16	1.20		
Chemicals	6.40	6.00	4.65	x	
Containers	1.07	0.82	1.03	x	
Drugs & Cosmetics	2.83	4.03	4.14		x
Elec. Equip. & Electronics (excl. TV & Radio)	4.02	5.05	6.32		x
Foods & Beverages	1.48	3.12	2.59	x	

MUTUAL FUNDS' PORTFOLIO DIVERSIFICATION
PERCENT OF TOTAL COMMON STOCK BY INDUSTRIES
1956–1961–1966

	1956	1961	1966	Estimated Changes, Including Other Institutions Higher	Lower
Financial (incl. Banks & Insurance)	8.32	14.24	8.33		
Machinery	2.01	1.31	0.93	x	
Metals & Mining	5.49	3.00	4.17		
Motion Pictures	0.18	0.19	0.13		
Natural Gas	3.72	2.44	1.06	x	
Office Equipment	1.97	5.50	6.69		x
Oil	17.76	9.95	12.58	x	
Paper	3.79	2.24	1.59	x	
Public Utilities (incl. Telephone)	9.28	11.73	10.29	x	
Railroad	4.68	2.64	2.64		
Railroad Equipment	0.36	0.16	0.38	x	
Retail Trade	1.90	3.45	2.52	x	
Rubber (incl. Tires)	3.36	1.89	1.41	x	
Steel	6.90	3.19	1.91		
TV & Radio	0.73	0.94	2.05		x
Textiles	0.23	0.48	0.84		
Tobacco	0.48	1.78	0.97	x	
Miscellaneous*	2.74	8.09	10.26		
Totals	100.00%	100.00%	100.00%		

* Includes diversified industrial companies not readily assignable to specific industry categories.

Note: Based on reports nearest to calendar year-end of the forty largest mutual funds as of December 31, 1966, whose total net assets represented 79.2 percent of total net assets of all institute member companies.

Let me emphasize that the proper utilization of this Profit-Aid depends on what kind of investment thinking might prevail in the future. You should not necessarily worry just because your stock or stocks are heavily held by the large portfolios. More times than not, this is a good sign. But do not be lulled into a false sense of security from this—as so many people are. Be aware of the risk which *can* exist when stocks are put away in large blocks and which represent a significant portion of most portfolios. The slightest change in thinking can cause managers to shrink the percentage representation, and this, indeed, is a cause for concern.

By the same token, you should look at the industries which are sparsely held, with a view toward possibly placing yourself in a favorable demand-supply position for the future. If you spot an area which is not currently appreciated by investment managers—but which you believe may be in years to come—you should realize that you have an extra point of strength going for you.

Thus, Profit-Aid 24 provides you with greater perspective for both defense and offense in your stock-owning "bag of tricks."

Chapter Twenty-four

Separating the Wheat from the Chaff in Statements by Corporate Officials

Later on (chapters 27 and 28) I will discuss the validity of brokerage firms' research bulletins and how to distinguish those which have somewhat prejudiced, poorly timed, or ill-conceived opinions. Most such bulletins are quite analytical and objective, however, and the great percentage are written with a sincere effort to separate attractive from unattractive investments.

In one of these same subsequent chapters (27), I also allude to the position of corporate management itself and the natural optimism which generally prevails here.

So, just as I endeavor to give you some "inside" facts of life about research reports, I want to alert you to some important warnings about certain public statements and forecasts made by corporate officials. Indeed, countless dollars have been lost simply because investors had blind faith in statements made by management of publicly held organizations.

As I see it, there are certain "sins" which occur over and over again and which tend to misinform or mislead (although generally without intention) the public. Let's consider some of these now:

1. *How rosy can you be?* Students of sociology are the first to state that we Americans are but puppets in the hands of Madison Avenue. Indeed, we are all influenced by professional advertising and public relations, and many of our buying habits are the way they are because of the efforts of hucksters. Knowing this, how can people be so gullible as to accept forecasts which are advertising-oriented as if they are objective, truly analytical, and unprejudiced?

   Take any industry which is sensitive to public psychology and which reacts rather violently to whether or not the public is in a "buying mood." Like automobiles, for example. An auto is a "durable" good: it is one which can be made to last longer if we choose to do so (a new paint job, new tires, a motor overhaul, and we have an item which should last for many, many more years). Since we can make an auto last and not feel the necessity of buying a new one, why do people do so in such huge quantities every year? Naturally, some autos get so old and tired that repair is uneconomical and thus there is a large number of them scrapped every year. In addition to this, there are really two reasons for purchase of new cars. The first of these reasons is obviously style. The cars with a rumble seat or the square look or the protruding fins simply lose their glamour and acceptance and the owners of cars with these features decide to update themselves and have what is really in style. The second reason for changing to a new car is even less tangible. It involves doing what others are doing—buying what and when others are buying—having a status symbol, "keeping up with the Joneses," treating ourselves to an extravagance for goodness-knows-what reason. Any number of intangible forces drive us, but we do know one thing: that we like to feel that others are doing it at the same time.

Don't think the advertising, marketing, and promotion experts for the automobile industry are blind to the importance of mass psychology. And that is why they are generally brimming with optimism each year about the prospects for new-car sales. They want to create the impression in the minds of the public that people *will* be buying, knowing that this in itself is an aid to their spending rationale. This is not to imply that these representatives of the new-car industry are dishonest. They are paid to do a job and they have no desire to harm anyone by doing so.

From the standpoint of the investor, however, such overoptimism can be harmful. One has to be extremely careful and not mistake rosy predictions which are intended to develop sales momentum for an objective appraisal of economics. Although the optimistic predictions will sometimes come true, just as often they will not.

Therefore, the investor in auto stocks or in stocks of companies which are sensitive to new-car sales (steel, glass, rubber, etc.) must take such prognostications with a grain of salt.

Naturally, the auto industry is not the only one which is subject to such psychological stimulation, but it serves as a good example of what can be expected in this day and age of hidden persuaders.

2. *How about companies making forecasts of sales and earnings?* Like a housewife, all companies have a budget on which they live. And just as a housewife has an idea what it will cost her to live next month, corporate officials gauge their expenditures according to what they visualize their income and overhead to be in the time ahead. As you can imagine, budgeting of any kind is anything but exact; in fact, most management experts will agree that it is really just an "educated stab in the dark." As a matter of fact, there are very few businesses which can estimate with a great deal of accuracy what will happen to income and expenses over the next twelve

months (utilities come closest to this exactitude). It is one thing for a company to forecast what this year's results will be in October or thereabouts, but it is an entirely different matter to do this early in the year. In fact, it may be downright foolhardy!

Which brings us to some important points in this discussion of corporate sins. First of all, I am extremely leery of companies which attempt to pinpoint earnings when the year has just begun. If you are anything but a salaried worker, you tell me what your income for the full year will be as early as January or February. If you can't do it with your personal income, you can imagine how difficult it must be for a corporation—which has innumerable products to sell and innumerable employees to pay—to come close. It is one thing for a company president to say that he expects current year's results "to continue the trend established in 19—" or that "given a decent overall economic climate, earnings should exceed those of last year." But to state unequivocally that "earnings for the present year should be $1.29 per share" is a sign either that the man doesn't understand business in general or that he is trying to promote and deceive. So watch for this pigheaded sign and avoid stocks which are represented by such management.

Secondly, watch out for any company which makes a forecast look like something scientific. It is one thing to say that "sales for the coming year should exceed ten million dollars," but it is another (and completely ridiculous) thing to say that "sales for the coming year will be $11,485,675.22." The latter figure looks so exact, scientific, and mathematical, but to me it looks like a smokescreen. Any forecast should be labeled as such, and the figures used should indicate their indefinite nature. I well remember just such an example, which occurred with a small company located in the San Francisco Bay Area. During the first few weeks in January of 1960 my phone must have rung thirty times with the same tune on the other end of the line. The company in mind had sent a letter to its stockholders with the specific purpose of informing them of management's forecast for the 1960 calendar year (the letter was dated December 30, 1959). The company stated that the forecast "indicates earnings of $1.75 per common share on a gross sales of $5,689,500 and profits—before taxes—of $1,562,750." Not bad for a stock selling at $6–7 a share, huh? I hit the roof! "How gullible can you be?" I asked my clients. Not only was the statement tainted (for one thing, the $1.75-per-share figure was based on shares held only by the public and excluded many hundreds of thousands of shares held by management) but also the whole idea of making such a precise forecast of sales and earnings for the full year ahead in a completely unproven business was complete foolishness. Besides which—it "smelled to high heaven."

I persuaded my inquirers to forget the matter. Obviously, others didn't, because within a few weeks the stock had risen to $8.50. But here the story ends—and just as you might (should) expect. Less than three years later, this stock had fallen to 6 . . . *cents,* that is. So you can see why I am adamant about this. Whenever you see such foolishness on the part of management, run for the exit. Avoid the stock if you don't already own it; sell it if you do.

3. *How accurate have previous estimates been?* In life we judge much by past performance. While the statement, "A leopard never changes his spots," is pretty narrow-minded, I think it is fair to say that a person's history runs pretty true. The same goes for corporate officials. The company president whose history shows he is always high in his earnings estimates and forecasts should certainly not be taken at his word in the future.

This is where experienced brokers and analysts can be very helpful. Their experience includes a memory of how certain companies are always conservative in their predictions, while others are always on the optimistic side. Needless to say, it is best to ignore the latter's statements. As a matter of fact, I think it is safe to say that you should ignore the stock altogether.

Instead, give me the company which bends over backwards to protect its stockholders and which plays down its forecasts. Give me the company which does not want to put air into its stock. Such an attitude is a reflection of management honesty and integrity and conservatism. And since a company is no better than the people who run it, give me these people I can trust implicitly and who have the wisdom to run their own business and not to run their stock.

4. *What about management which talks about its own stock?* Occasionally I run across a letter or statement written by a high company official in which the latter discusses his stock's recent decline. Or in which he mentions and refutes some pessimistic gossip which has come to his ears. These, too, are definite signs of weakness, to my way of thinking. A legitimate company isn't concerned about its stock's daily market action and/or idle gossip which might prevail, because it knows that its performance (in increasing sales and earnings) will determine its success. It is the company which is worried about its own performance and which is afraid the public will discover its weakness and flimsiness that feels compelled to defend itself against petty talk or against panicky, uninformed selling in the market.

5. *How about the treatment of nonrecurring profits?* One last clue to corporate integrity shows up in how occasional windfalls are treated by management in their statements to the world. Every so often a company will receive some extraordinary income, perhaps from the sale of a building or other asset or perhaps for the return of income taxes paid, etc. The main thing about these is that they are *not* recurring—and they should be treated as such. The company which lumps such nonrecurring income in with operating income to make a good show-

ing is involved in a deceitful practice and you should not want to have anything to do with it. So watch for this sin, too, in assessing corporate management.

Conclusion

All of the above once again sounds skeptical. Fortunately these sins reflect the exception rather than the rule. Most corporate management is honest and hard-working and would not think of engaging in any of the above. But, in this book, I want to prepare you for anything, and I want you to avoid any of the above, which would, I am sure, cost you some dollars over the years. Remember, there are so many fine, legitimate "fish in the sea." Who needs the others?

To summarize, our Profit-Aid 25 includes the following advice:

1. *Do not accept forecasts from "psychological-stimulation" industries as the gospel.*
2. *Beware of companies attempting precise forecasts for themselves early in the year.*
3. *Consider how reliable management has been in the past in its forecasts.*
4. *Avoid stocks in which management is too conscious of their own market fluctuations.*
5. *Avoid stocks in which management has not separated nonrecurring profits from operating profits.*

Chapter Twenty-five

Distinguishing Productive Research and Development in a Growth Company

.

One of the magic words of the postwar period has been the expression "R&D." This term, which is simply an abbreviation for the words "research and development," has taken on huge proportions in recent years. The reason, of course, is that R&D is the backbone of so many companies' futures—the secret to success, no less. I know I do not have to labor the whys of this statement. It is obvious that the companies which bring out the new products of the future are the ones which stand a superior chance for growth—and new products are invariably the result of long and tedious research-and-development work.

Because of this, many analysts and investors have come to regard any company which spends large amounts on R&D as a "growth" company. Naturally, this is not the case. Many companies have come to the sad realization in recent years that they have "R&D'ed" themselves into some pretty big losses. Research is an out-of-pocket expense and it reduces profits directly; it is an investment in the future and it has to pay off in the form of new products or developments which in

175

turn produce sales and net income. Ineffective research is, in essence, money poured "down a rathole."

The main purpose of this discussion is to warn you against associating heavy R&D expenditures directly with future growth. The last statement about ineffective research is almost unnecessary. I know I don't have to tell you to analyze the *quality* of a company's research in assessing its importance. The organization which has been able to bring new products to market consistently and with success is the one which should command a large research plus. The proof of the pudding is the result, not just the expenditure alone.

But R&D is a calculated gamble which is hard to analyze. The drug industry is a perfect example of this gamble. A company may go along for a few years without any major breakthrough and suddenly, just when you have come to the conclusion that its R&D is relatively ineffective, emerge with an important discovery and corresponding new-product development. Or you might incorrectly assess a company's R&D efficiency because success has not been startling, failing to realize that certain important research programs were commenced only in the past few years (success does not bloom overnight; as a matter of fact, the average new product takes five to seven years to get from its initial research stage to the marketplace).

Still, the theory remains that if a company spends so much money each year on R&D, eventually something should come of it. And thus many people contend that R&D alone is a sound criterion of a growth vehicle. One strong argument against this theory is that *large R&D expenditures may simply be a form of survival for a company*. The ethical drug industry is just such an example. An outfit which rests on its laurels and on its existing products, without preparing for the future, will be out of business before long. Patents run out in time and, most important, new developments make accepted products obsolete. Therefore, you cannot look at large R&D expenses by the industry itself and assume that this guarantees growth. It should be obvious in this case that the large research expenses are a matter of survival. Substantial growth may follow—and then again, it may not. And some companies may experience substantial progress while others are going downhill. When you do spot a company which is spending far more than its competitors on R&D, it may well be an important clue—and you should be alert to the prospects—but you do have to consider the Big Picture and place it all within the proper framework of reference.

So that you are not confused by R&D figures, I thought it would be helpful if I showed you which industries are noted for spending large sums looking for new developments. Like the drug example, these industries utilize research as a combination of battle for survival and search for unprecedented growth. In all cases, it is a matter of finding the most efficient research spenders in order to pull the true growth companies, if any, out of the group. Incidentally, rather than use flat dollar amounts, which would make the largest industries look like the major growth areas, it is common practice to use the gauge of "Research as a Percentage of Sales." This gives you a far better idea of the relative importance, and it is the presentation of these figures, which constitute Profit-Aid 26, which should prove useful to you. (See page 178.)

One technical bit of warning. There is a very thin line between where R&D stops and where general engineering work begins. It is hard to separate research-and-development work from the normal preparation of existing products. Research of the kind to which we should be especially attracted is that which is devoted to the betterment of present products or to the conception of new ideas. This is certainly investment in the future by the company doing it. The general engineering which might, for example, be devoted to the actual manufacture of items is necessary and it is important, but it lacks the future explosiveness of what we have defined as research work. Thus, it is important that you feel certain that the R&D which is presented to you as a strong plus factor is really R&D and not general engineering. Hopefully, your brokerage concern's analysts will do this job of separation for you, and my

COST OF R&D PERFORMANCE AS PERCENT OF NET SALES;
SELECTED INDUSTRIES, 1957, 1960, AND 1964

Industry	1957	1960	1964
All industries	3.4%	4.2%	4.4%
Aircraft and missiles	16.8	22.9	26.6
Communications equipment and electronic components	N.C.	12.9	12.5
Scientific and mechanical measuring instruments	9.5	10.8	9.4
Optical, surgical, photographic, and other instruments	5.2	5.6	7.3
Other electrical equipment	N.C.	9.2	7.2
Industrial chemicals	5.0	5.8	4.9
Drugs and medicines	3.6	4.6	4.7
Machinery	3.4	4.6	4.2
Other chemicals	1.3	2.3	2.3
Rubber products	1.7	2.0	2.0
Stone, clay, and glass products	N.C.	1.7	1.8
Petroleum refining and extraction	.7	1.1	1.0
Primary metals	.5	.8	.8

N.C.: Not comparable.
Source: National Science Foundation, "Basic Research, Applied Research and Development in Industry, 1964," by Leland J. Haworth.

mention here is really intended for these people rather than for you (assuming you are the layman investor and not a professional).

At any rate, I hope the importance of R&D has been made clear, and I especially hope that you are aware of the distinction of research which will provide substantial growth for the company you are considering and research which might be a necessity for survival. Once again, there can be a thin line in distinguishing one from the other, but the idea should now be firmly planted in your mind, so that you can make a more intelligent appraisal of what constitutes a growth investment.

Chapter Twenty-six

Inventories:
A Key to Success and Failure

Every good businessman is extremely conscious of the quantity and quality of goods he is carrying on his shelf. These goods—his inventories—are the key to his future; if they are well-conceived, salable goods they will generate sales and profits, and they will be converted into all-important dollars. If, on the other hand, the goods are not well conceived and not too salable, then they may be worth a good deal less than the value for which they are carried on the company's books. When the company comes to this realization, it will have to write down these assets, and such reevaluation can be disastrous.

Just how disastrous these writedowns can be is almost unbelievable. Consider the cases of Ampex Corporation and Transitron, Inc. Both companies were considered by security analysts and investors at one time to be prime growth outfits. Their records showed consistent increases in sales and large advances in net income. The only trouble was that neither company had, at one time in its corporate life, taken a realistic attitude toward inventories on its shelves. Both went merrily along selling what they sold, while at the same time turning their backs and closing their eyes to that which was *un*sold. Then came the day of reckoning for both. In the case of Ampex, new management took over and faced up to the fact that considerable inventory was just plain obsolete and naturally worth very little—and far less than its carrying value on the books. At the time of reassessment, it was determined that inventory was overvalued by many millions of dollars. After the writedown the company ended up with a loss of ten million dollars (before tax savings). Interestingly enough, this loss was more than half the money Ampex had made during its whole corporate life. So what had appeared to be a profitable and growing company was really not one at all. In the meantime, Ampex stock had dropped from its 1959 high of 45⅝ to levels in the $10–15 range.

The Transitron experience was even worse. Without going into great detail, Transitron's inventory evaluation converted what once looked to be a very successful and profitable concern into the complete opposite. This realization was enough to force Transitron's market price from a high of 60 in 1960 to as low as 6¼ in 1963.

It should be obvious from this that the security analyst who is studying a company has to be extremely conscious of inventories. Too often this important area is overlooked, or at least not given the weight it deserves.

In discussing inventory policy as a clue to the future, I have highlighted examples of high evaluation; needless to say, low evaluation signifies inherent strengths, since:

1. You don't have the worry of drastic writedowns.
2. The company in mind is probably *under*stating its net income. The fact that a company is attaching the very minimum costs to inventory means that very large amounts are being charged off currently to Cost of Goods Sold. As the low-cost goods on the shelf are sold, reported profits should rise considerably. Your understanding of this will allow you to buy the company's

stock before these profits are reported, and you stand to benefit handsomely thereby.

Thus, you, as a potential reader of research reports and as a separator of good from bad investments, should be well aware of whether the analysts have done their homework correctly. This is just one more little-thought-of detail which can be ever so important. In short, your awareness of *inventory evaluation* can screen out the "weak sisters" and aid you in understanding better the exploding companies of tomorrow.

Part Three

Establishing a Profitable Relationship with Your Stockbroker

Chapter Twenty-seven

Separating the Gullible
Broker from the Astute

This section of the book is designed to show you how to out-analyze the analysts and how to locate and work with the right broker. It contains many methods and safeguards for your protection and enrichment.

When you hear what the initial safeguard is, you will think that I consider people in my business completely naïve. Obviously, this is not the case. Most are bright and practical and not easily fooled. But there are some who do not fall in this category, and I want to prepare you to spot these and naturally to discard their ideas.

As the investment business grew during the post-World War II period, many new people became brokers, analysts, salesmen, salesmen-analysts, etc. With greater interest and greater activity in the market, there grew a greater quest for information from corporate officials. As I have hinted before, it is a mistake to accept naturally prejudiced opinions of corporate officials as "the gospel." While some managements are very conservative in their approach with security analysts, it is unusual not to find management bubbling with enthusiasm about their prospects. Alas, if they are not bubbling with confidence and optimism, they can't be very aggressive. (What top-flight, want-to-get-ahead guy will stick with a company he thinks is going downhill?)

Despite this fact of life, there are countless analysts and security salesmen who are victimized by their own gullibility. I know, for example, of certain people in my business who expect to get reliable information by telephone from corporate officials who don't know them "from Adam." Now, put yourself in the position of the corporate official who receives a sudden phone call from a completely unknown person who represents an unknown brokerage firm. How much information would you give this stranger? Very little, if any, I would say. And what you might give him could just be slightly deceptive, unless you happen to be a complete idealist. It is unbelievable to me how many people fail to realize this prejudiced response—how many people fail to discern between good and completely unreliable information. It is essential to picture the corporate official correctly. Perhaps he is a pinnacle of integrity—but most probably he is prejudiced when it comes to his own company. The truth no doubt is that the man on the other end of the telephone is a large stockholder in his company and that he certainly does not want his holdings to diminish in value. To expect an objective and completely truthful answer may be asking too much!

I will never, never forget some experiences learned (the hard way) by some analysts I knew. During the scrambling market of 1961 these people had formed the habit of telephoning companies throughout the United States to learn of earnings forecasts and company developments. For a while in 1961 the market on small companies was rising almost without regard for fundamentals. The market, in short, had become a "One-Way Street"—a speculative binge which, despite 1967's similar experience, has to be classified as very, very unusual. Markets such as this create bad habits, some of which are never broken. Such was the case with two specific issues, which should serve as good examples for us.

One stock was an electronics manufacturer in Massachusetts and the other was a Florida-based builder of missile bases. The first stock was selling in the $50–60 price range, the second in the $20–28 area. Both stocks were strongly recommended by certain brokers *based on telephone conversations with corporate officials.* Telephone conversations *AND NOTHING MORE.* This in itself was flimsy enough for me, and I warned these brokers that they might be "playing with fire." This became especially apparent by the market action of the two stocks. Despite heavy buying of these stocks by the brokers, their market prices were edging lower and lower. Now my conservative approach became more than just a caution. "Look," I said to one of the brokers involved (a friendly competitor), "don't you think perhaps someone has spun you a line? I know the 'facts' which have been presented to you. But I can't believe that you, residing some three thousand miles away from both Massachusetts and Florida, can know so much about these companies from your phone conversations. My analysis is that the people who are selling these stocks [and there was obviously considerable selling, since the stocks were declining while these brokers were buying large amounts] know more about what is really going on than you do. Indeed, I conclude that these sellers know something that you do not know—and that you are therefore 'barking up the wrong tree.' "

But flexibility was not a trait of these individuals. In essence, I think they *wanted* to believe the stories which had been told them so badly that they actually did believe them.

The end of these tales is anything but pleasant. The electronics-company stock fell from $50–60 to the $10–15 range within a year's time, and the missile-site contractor plummeted from the $20–28 figure to $2 in the same rapid succession.

What is my advice to you, based on these reverse Horatio Alger stories? Mainly I want you to *know how information presented to you has been obtained. Know whether your advisors are really well informed or whether they are, instead, the victims of scuttlebutt or of misinformation.* Make sure that recommendations are based on good factual information and that no one has been carried away with enthusiasm to the point of ignorance. Beware of naïve and gullible brokers. Do *without* their flimsy judgment.

Chapter Twenty-eight

Research Reports—
Their Functions, Advantages, and Dangers

The New York Stock Exchange has advertised for many years. The Exchange feels that one of its obligations is to educate the public and one of its key phrases has been: "Investigate before you invest." This is, naturally, good advice. But most investors either do not take the time or are ill-prepared to do a thorough job of investigation. Besides which, most are confused and do not know where to go to find out about management, new products, competition, and all the essential considerations one should entertain in analyzing a company.

If a person has the inclination to dig out the necessary facts himself, he has a world of information at his disposal. Aside from personal observation (of new products, for example), the investor can do his "homework" by reading any of a multitude of statistical services. In addition, he can learn a great deal about a company by reading its annual report. Or he can ask his broker if his firm has published a research report on the industry or company in mind. Actually, this latter tool— the brokerage-firm research study—can be the most useful. As a matter of fact, such reports are responsible for most decisions made by individual investors and are often instrumental in bringing about a stock's near-term rise or decline.

In just a minute I am going to give you some important warnings about these research bulletins, but before I do I think it will be helpful for you to know research procedure in a brokerage concern. You would be amazed to learn how much money some brokers spend for research every year. For example, our company spends many hundreds of thousands of dollars a year on this service, as do many, many major firms. Aside from having security analysts (twenty to fifty is not unusual), you can imagine the expenses incurred through making field trips, phone calls, etc.—all in an effort to bring profitable ideas to customers. Because these reports come from specialists, it stands to reason that people react to the recommendations. Needless to say, these reports should never be accepted blindly as the gospel; as a matter of fact, there are significant dangers involved in following some of these recommendations. So now I am going to give you some warnings—and some advice on how to use and *not* to use research reports.

Let me preface the discussion by saying that this is not an effort to make a financial analyst out of you, although we have already discussed the guideposts to follow in determining whether a company and an industry and a specific stock constitute a good buy for you. Actually, the best way to tear apart a research report to determine its validity is to follow these guideposts. What I want to do now is to give you some hints and advice that you seldom, if ever, hear discussed. In other words, we are now entering the skeleton closet of security analysis. I think you will come out of this closet as a more sophisticated stock buyer.

Here are my clues:

1. *Always determine the tone of the writer and cast aside those reports which are "pushy."* While a person who has a flare for writing can't (and shouldn't) hold himself back and become dull as dishwater, a person who

has the facts to back up his judgment does not have to resort to promotional tactics. A top research report will read like a well-written list of instructions: it will take you from beginning to end in a logical pattern and then show you simply why the security represents sound value. I have seen too many reports that read like flashy advertisements, and I feel strongly that the investor should file these in the wastebasket. Just as in any other field, avoid the person who pushes too hard.

2. *Determine whether the report you are reading is the result of some personal contact with the company analyzed.* You read a research report to get some original thinking and to get up-to-date facts and information. Conditions within an industry or a company can change quite rapidly. I always say to my clients that I never expect to be the very first to know when such changes occur, but I most certainly do not want to be among the last to know, either.

I feel much more secure reading a study which states openly that management of the company analyzed has been visited and interviewed at length. This takes a lot of guesswork away and makes you feel more confident about earnings and other conditions and forecasts.

3. *Read between the lines and analyze whether the writer has considered the Big Picture involving the industry or company.* In other words, has he considered the basic positives and negatives and has he considered what the future holds? And has he not fallen into the trap of the inevitable cycles discussed in Chapter 21?

I am not trying to plant feelings of unrest into your mind about the securities business. I am only preparing you better to separate legitimate, completely objective research studies from those which might be prompted by other considerations. You see, the best security analysts are skeptics at heart, and I am only conditioning you in this way.

Before closing this discussion of research reports and recommendations, we should consider the most important point of all—*that you should beware when certain stocks suddenly become widely recommended by brokers everywhere.*

The Danger of Unanimous Opinion!

In the stock market we are taught to think independently and objectively. Human nature remains the same, however, and it is hard to sit back and resist a trend when it takes hold. While we men like to think that it is only the weaker sex which is subject to style changes and other fads and emotional clamorings, I think it is safe to say that both sexes engage in mass movements. (How many double-breasted suits did you discard all at once?) A sudden urge to run to the store and buy a hula hoop because everyone else has one will cost you only a dollar and never get you in trouble, but "hula-hoop buying" in the stock market can cost you many dollars. This brings us to Profit-Aid 27, which is: *Whenever an industry group or an individual stock suddenly becomes a universal favorite and is the subject of research reports by a multitude of brokers, it should be a cause for suspicion.*

There are many stocks which have been accepted as good investments for many, many years by brokers and other financial advisors. Minnesota Mining, Eastman Kodak, IBM, and Corning Glass are typical favorites, and it is seldom that you will see any negative research reports on such companies. I am *not* worried about the unanimity of opinion of these! What I am worried about is when brokers *suddenly* hop on the bandwagon of an unproven industry or company.

Perhaps you're thinking: "Why should I be worried when brokers are all suggesting XYZ Company for purchase? Shouldn't their recommendations keep people buying XYZ stock and shouldn't this buying keep the stock going up in price? This thinking is logical—but really not completely practical.

I continually emphasize the importance of original thinking in the market. If you can spot a trend in an industry or in a company before that trend develops, you stand to make big money. I gave you many examples of this "look-ahead" thinking in Chapters 1 and 2. If you wait for the trend to develop, you will be late in buying and will have missed a great deal of capital appreciation. Besides which, just as you were unable to spot the trend until it developed and became a reality, maybe you do not realize that the trend is almost over. Remember, too, that the investors who had the foresight to recognize the trend before its realization *HAVE BEEN WAITING TO SELL UPON ITS REALIZATION.*

Thus, the rash of research reports has created high prices and the shrewd investor takes advantage of this opportunity to sell to the latecomers. This astute stock buyer knows that the maximum gains have already been made. What he wants to do is cast his eyes on greener pastures—where the public has *not* yet participated.

So you can see why I am skeptical of sudden unanimous thinking. In the majority of cases (the exceptions are the basic industries or companies which qualify under the tests I pointed out in Chapter 5) this unanimity of opinion translated into a heavy supply of research recommendations merely creates the buying for which the farsighted investor has been waiting—to sell.

Conclusion

The conclusion here is obvious. Get all the information you can, but be a hardboiled judge of what you read. Use the research materials available to you, but keep in mind my warning about them. In short, you know just one more fact of investment life, and I believe you are now in a better position to make the right decisions based on research reports.

Chapter Twenty-nine

How to Work With Your Broker; What to Expect and What Not to Expect from Him; How to Choose a Broker

Most individuals seem to be satisfied and content with one (general) doctor, one attorney, one dentist, one (personal) CPA—so much so that professional, if not personal, relationships with these people generally last for many years. Why, then, do so many people have two or more stockbrokers *at the same time*—and feel a need to switch brokers numerous times over their investment lives? In short, why do so many feel a rapport and a sense of loyalty to the first group of "service" professionals and not carry out this same principle when it comes to their stock investing?

Naturally, there are many reasons for this difference in attitude, so many that I will not bore you with a lengthy exploration. Yet I deem it essential that you realize that:

1. This lack of rapport, respect, and loyalty is usually the fault of *both* parties.
2. The absence of a close relationship is to the detriment of the investor (and, of course, the broker).

3. The existence of a doctor-patient, attorney-client relationship *can* be achieved—to the distinct advantage of the investor.

Needless to say, an untold number of mistakes have been made over the years by both stockbrokers and clients simply because the two failed to understand one another. Since mistakes in the market are costly, it is my hope to eliminate what, in my opinion, has been a substantial stumbling block for many in the achievement of the ultimate goal of making money. By the end of this chapter, you should know what to expect and what not to expect from your advisor; you should recognize methods of getting better service; and you should understand how to work *with,* rather than against, your broker. A real understanding of this may do as much for your investment success in the future as all the stock-market books put together! Thus, I consider the rest of this chapter as a Profit-Aid. It is our final one, number 28, to be specific.

Realizing the Limitations of an Advisor
Before delving into this subject, let me make it clear that I am not president, or even a member, of the Society for the Prevention of Cruelty to Brokers. If anything, I am critical of my profession. Therefore, the listing of limitations is no defense for mediocre performance and is instead intended as a bridge to overcome the communication gap which so often hampers success. Here are some pertinent limitations:

1. *The difficulty of judging where the overall market is going.* Since a market trend has so much to do with the performance of individual stocks, it is probably frightening to many to realize the difficulty one has in forecasting what lies ahead for the general market. The limitations, however, are great in such forecasting. Whereas I discussed this earlier, there is no harm in repeating such problem factors as:

a. What lies ahead for the domestic economy.
b. What lies ahead for the world economy.

   c. Political developments at home and abroad.

   d. Monetary considerations in the United States and throughout the world.

   e. Overall psychology of investors.

Needless to say, the assessment of these factors carries great risks. As if points a through d were not enough, the determination of e is enough to make one throw up his hands in frustration. As you know, the public is fickle, and history has shown how many times sentiment suddenly turns one way or another, for no apparent reason, and how even the most drastic efforts to alter thinking can have little or no effect.

Secondly, all the logical assessment possible can be "thrown out the window" by some completely unexpected development. The examples of our 1962 Cuban struggle and President Kennedy's assassination in 1963 discussed in Chapter 12 are typical.

Thus, do not expect miracles from your broker. He should have an opinion of some sort as to the market's general trend, but the chances are that his selection of individual securities within the market is going to be more accurate than his opinion of the market as a whole.

2. *Realize a broker's inability to pinpoint near-term performance of anything.* Just as it is difficult to judge overall trends, it is ridiculous to expect judgment of the near-term action either of the general market or of individual stocks. Despite this, I wonder how many thousands of times a year brokers all over the country are asked the question: "Shall I buy it now or wait a few days?" or "Shall I wait till the end of the week to sell it?"

Not only does the stock market often interpret news and near-term developments exactly opposite from what you might expect (thereby complicating assessment), but also a person can be so right in his fundamental judgment of something and be so wrong in his timing—for reasons which are totally unpredictable. The Brunswick-American Machine and Foundry situation discussed in Chapter 1 is typical of this and typical of so many situations. Certainly you would have been dead right in your analysis that the bowling twins were doomed to difficulty, but you could have looked mighty silly for a while. You might well have concluded that trouble lay ahead for both companies and sold your stock out only to see it rise ten or twenty or thirty points higher after your sale. And why? Because you were wrong? No! Simply because other people did *not* have the foresight to analyze the situation correctly. Needless to say, I never base my investment decisions on the prayer that others will misanalyze. As the famous comedian Lew Lehr used to say: "Monkeys is the craziest people." When it comes to investments, sometimes "people is the craziest monkeys," but this is something you should not expect or count on.

3. *Realize the difficulty of advising if your objectives, personality, and temperament are not known by your broker.* At the beginning of this chapter I compared a person's approach to investing with approach to a doctor, lawyer, dentist, or accountant. You cannot expect a good job from any of these professionals unless you open up some of your past and particularly acquaint them with your current problems. The same goes for your broker. Make sure he knows your objectives (i.e., is current income of importance to you, how soon will you be depending on your investments for retirement or for other purposes, how much will you be investing yearly, etc.). Furthermore, make sure he understands your personality and temperament.

The latter may appear silly to you, but a broker's understanding of you as a person is ever so important. If you are the nervous type, for example, he should know it. If you are a poor loser, he should know it. If you are extraemotional, let him in on it. If you hide these things from him, you are limiting the understanding between the two of you and are hindering your chances for success.

4. *Realize the inevitability of occasional losses in your investments.* Just as Willie Mays knows that out of every three trips to the plate he is destined (over a long period of time) to make an out about twice, a stockbroker has limitations against which he is going to be relatively helpless. Stock

markets fluctuate both ways, and a person investing year after year is bound to invest once in a while at a high point. By corollary, investing at a high point means that a lower point is bound to follow, which is simply a complicated way of saying that losses will exist. What is a high point today, however, may not be such in the future. In well-chosen investments, time has a way of bringing about success. Thus, just be sure you are invested in well-situated companies and do not fret and do not criticize your broker for a wait which may be forced upon you.

The assumption here, however, is that the basic choice has been good—which is naturally not always the case. Brokers are human and, as such, are prone to err on occasions. Every —but *every*—broker has a few skeletons in his closet, and you must not assume your account representative to be incompetent if one of these mistakes falls upon you. A series of these constitutes a sign for caution and further exploration by you, but an occasional loss is hardly grounds for switching brokers.

So much for limitations as they might affect you. In order to achieve the ultimate, I have now compiled a number of dos and don'ts which should accomplish the following: (a) enable you to do a better job of choosing the right broker for you; (b) help you close the communication gap which is bound to exist at the beginning; (c) establish the proper relationship between you and your broker, so that the two of you can derive maximum performance.

Here are the dos:

1. Do determine whether the broker has a *philosophy* regarding investments. If you get the impression he is going to suggest frequent changes and a great deal of buying and selling, go on to someone else. Get someone who has a long-range philosophy, both with regard to the stocks he recommends and with regard to his desire to grow with you.
2. Do see if he follows a logical pattern, i.e., whether he wants you eventually to have representation in certain

industry groups, whether he insists that you lay a foundation with solid stocks before you speculate, and whether he is giving thought to *your* problems. Avoid the person who has a "hit-and-miss" system, without establishing a pattern and a philosophy for you to follow.

3. Do determine whether the individual has the time to supervise your holdings on a consistent basis.

4. Do let him know (if you make this decision) that he is *your* man and that you will be loyal to him as long as the account is handled well and as long as you feel he still has your interests at heart.

5. Do "check in" occasionally; that is, make an appointment for a *short* visit once or twice a year, or accomplish the same communication by phone every three months or so. While this may sound in conflict with some of the above (isn't it inconsistent to want a broker who has the time to handle your account—and then to be the one who has to check in to him?), the fact is that some of the best brokers are not the "pushy" type and/or are busy people who may need a push from you to get a little more than ordinary attention.

Now for the don'ts:

1. Don't place the feeling of pressure upon your broker to produce. As mentioned, most investments take patience, and pressure on a broker who has your best interests at heart may force him to take a shorter-term approach. A good broker realizes, without your telling him, that it is his job to show profits over the years. But a "must-produce" attitude on your part can only create a barrier of a sort between you and make him tense; such tension and pressure can actually lead to poor selection on his part. In other words, once you have found a broker who is honest, has ability, and has an interest in you, have faith in him. And, just as you would not go to your doctor and say, "Cure me in one week or I'm going to

another doctor," do not set down any ultimatums to your stockbroker.

2. Don't use too many brokers. An investor with a very large account may find the need for a few advisors, but this is the exception. To my way of thinking, there are numerous reasons for not depending on more than one advisor, namely:

   a. Your inquiry of one broker about another's suggestion will probably tend to confuse you. Each broker has his own favorite stocks, and the reaction to what is obviously someone else's suggestion is liable to meet with a tone of disapproval, or at least an attitude of "Well, that's a decent stock, but I like _____ better." Furthermore, and of greater importance, there is a strong likelihood that Broker B will not know the pertinent reasons behind Broker A's recommendation. Since we can know only so many companies in depth, you may be accepting the shallow opinion of one broker on a recommendation which is known in depth by another.

   b. A broker gets to know when his client is doing business elsewhere. This may lead to:

      i. A "drying up" of good information and suggestions to you, the client. After all, a broker with the best type of research and information behind him is jealous of this. Certainly he does not want his competition getting credit for that which should be his—and thus he avoids opening up to the client who he fears is going to turn around and inform another broker.

      ii. A pressure to "sell" you, perhaps before he wants to. Let's face it, a broker is in business to do business. If client Mr. A now has ten thousand dollars "idle," he has no pressure to put this to work if he knows Mr. A is loyal and is not going to spend it with another broker. If he knows Mr. A "shops around," however, he will not want to lose the potential commission and will feel the pressure to sell him *now*.

3. Don't second-guess your broker. Either have faith in him and in his judgment or find another person to handle your account. Second-guessing does neither of you any good.

4. Don't limit your broker to price in a security he suggests for purchase or sale. Price limits in close proximity to the current market (as opposed to those used in the event the market takes a very sharp drop, as illustrated in Chapter 12) make bad sense both philosophically and arithmetically. If a stock is attractive for purchase at $20, it must also be attractive at $21; after all, if it is slated to double in price over a given period, what difference does it make whether you pay $20 or $21 (it is going to be a good investment in either case). Arithmetically, the idea of saving a fraction when you might lose many points by missing the opportunity just doesn't make sense. Looked at another way, you have to save a multitude of fractions in order to make up for the one decent missed opportunity brought about by insisting on saving the fraction.

5. Don't phone your broker too often. Do not drive him crazy with questions and opinions. Naturally, if you are a sizable account and are making frequent buying-and-selling decisions, you will have to be in touch with your representative continuously. But, for the normal, relatively inactive account to call daily is going to wear thin after a while. Perhaps the best rule is to call when you really have something pertinent to talk about. Naturally, the word "pertinent" is the key here. In my opinion, however, calling each time the market dips five to ten points is hardly pertinent talk.

But Who?

All of the above deals with the establishment of a better relationship between you and your broker. It makes one all-important assumption: that you have been able to find a person as your broker in whom you have confidence and with whom you are satisfied.

But what if you have not found your own little Bernard Baruch. What then? How do you find one, and what qualities should you use in your criterion for choosing the right person?

Needless to say, the success of other people may lead you to the right individual. If not, you should know the important considerations. While the gay divorcée or the young widow may rank good looks and personality high on their list, I am confining myself to investments here, and I would list three crucial traits, namely:

1. Knowledge (of the business).
2. Judgment.
3. Imagination.

Naturally, you want a broker who has made a student of himself and who has developed a knowledge in depth of the securities business; this, of course, includes an interest in economics as well as a foundation in industries, companies, the stock market, etc. Knowledge, however, is only a part of this stock-investing game. Some people know all the trivia and never master that intangible "feel" which leads to the maximum in money-making. Judgment is the key; satisfy yourself that the broker under the microscope gets a high rating here. And lastly, get yourself a broker who has imagination, who is not in such a rut that he can't get out of his own way, who is flexible enough to realize that markets change and that the paths to success ten years ago may not be the ones which fit into the patterns forming for the future.

Certainly you want to deal with a person whose personality blends with yours. In this respect, you just might need someone who complements or balances your own personality. In other words, if you are prone to make emotional decisions, for goodness' sake get yourself a broker who can tone

you down—one who has enough wisdom to keep you from loading up on Happy Jack Uranium. As a matter of fact, most people are best off dealing with a person who is conservative by nature. (Some of the best investments I know of started off as fairly conservative investments anyway.)

In addition to individual traits, your choice must include assessment of the brokerage firm with which you will be dealing. Is it a real investment house or is it a typical trading operation, thriving on fast plays and many changes in its clients' portfolios (i.e., many commissions)? Naturally, you should check to see whether your chosen firm is financially solvent itself. New York Stock Exchange member firms have stringent requirements, and the Exchange has brought in certain protections for clients in the event of a member firm's failure, but you can still ask to see a financial statement. Certainly, this is a "must" in the case of a smaller firm or of one which is not a member of the Big Board.

Most important, what kind of research does the firm have? Does it employ a broad staff of analysts who spend their time digging into the various industry groups and who are constantly contacting corporate management to give themselves up-to-date and (hopefully) well-informed views? Or are they instead a hit-and-miss, shallow outfit which is depending on luck or seat-of-the-pants judgment in their recommendations?

One last word here! Be careful of the firms which consistently emphasize your use of stop-loss orders for stocks they recommend. Stop-loss orders are basically for traders and speculators, not for investors. And brokers who encourage their use are in a way saying that they do not have the basic confidence in their own research and their own recommendations. If I am convinced that Bristol-Myers, for example, is a good buy *and if I have done the proper homework on this industry and on the company,* a ten-percent decline (ten percent is the percentage many brokers use as a suggestion for stop-loss orders) should only create an opportunity *to buy more,* not to sell myself out. Once again, the broker utilizing

the "sell-quick-if-it-doesn't-perform-quick" approach is generally lacking the kind of depth research which is the key to success in this business of ours.

Conclusions

I have seen little written on this rather touchy subject of finding, keeping, and getting the most out of relationships with stockbrokers. Naturally, this is all a very personal affair, and it is difficult to generalize. It would be easy to paint the picture of the ideal broker, but this image would change from person to person. I do believe, however, that enough solid advice has been given wherein you have a proper framework around which you can now operate—and operate more successfully.

Part Four

Conclusions

Chapter Thirty

Some Final Advice
and a Summary of Profit-Aids

Naturally, there is little sense in repeating all that has been spelled out in the preceding chapters. Yet, as the author, I cannot help but want to throw in my last "two cents' worth." The twenty-nine chapters cover a lot of ground but, most important, they are selective. Rather than scatter our thinking into hundreds of areas, most of which would never be useful to you, I have taken a "rifle" approach and pinpointed those topics which can be put to work now and which are definitely profit-oriented. My main objective has been to provide you with ideas, principles, and tools which are completely *practical* and, above all, *useful* to a large number of people.

Needless to say, investing in the stock market cannot be put into an empirical formula. Despite the increasing use of computers, success will never be achieved by mathematical computations alone. For one thing, machines cannot predict the future and, after all, it is what lies ahead which will determine stock prices. Furthermore, market values are always going to be determined by what human beings make them to be, and thus human emotions and psychology are going to be heavily involved.

With this in mind, I am the first to admit that security analysis (and just plain investing in the stock market) is definitely an *in*exact science, if it is a science at all. There are doctors in all fields of medicine, however, who will tell you that their profession is not all that exact, either. And this does not deter them from studying more and spending more time to make themselves more efficient and more exact, nor does it deter people needing medical aid or advice from seeking them out.

Actually, this book should accomplish the same kind of objectives—making *you* more exact, more proficient (and healthier), in your stock investing.

As mentioned a number of times, it is my conviction that a logical approach, though oftentimes simple, offers you the best chance for success. Thus, I have attempted to combine some of the technical aspects of our business with some real (hopefully, well-thought-out) common sense—and I am convinced that you will be a far better investor with this combination. In short, I have tried to build you a solid defense by making you a better judge of all you will be reading and all that will be presented to you over the years; and I have bolstered the "middle of your line" by showing you how to avoid some costly mistakes (made consistently by others) in the market. Most important, I have built what I consider a potent offense for you, strictly geared to the goal of making money in the market.

While only a small part of the advice given lent itself to the kind of summary advanced in our individual Profit-Aids, I think it may be useful to list the main thought of each before I close off with some final remarks. Here are the various Aids, with their reference pages shown:

Profit-Aids

Reference Page

1. Always consider what lies *ahead* for the industry and company in which you have your money;

Finale

To conclude, I want to emphasize that I have not held back any "punches" and have perhaps been too frank in spots. My conviction is strong, however, and I am convinced that a person should "get religion," even in the stock market. I hope the philosophy has been made clear and I am convinced that your assimilation of this plus the other materials, aids, and guides presented will increase your chances for success to a very large degree.

Good luck to you!

Appendix:
Industry-Rating Guide

As mentioned in Chapter 1, it is essential for investors to think along industry patterns and to determine which groups deserve higher or lower ratings than currently afforded by the investment community. These rating assessments are the key to buy-and-sell decisions—and their proper utilization can lead to uncovering the glamour issues of tomorrow.

Any use of the Rating Guide which follows should be made specifically in conjunction with Chapter 1—as well as, of course, with the kind of advice advanced throughout this book. As mentioned in the first chapter, I have divided the basic industries available for investment into 5, 4, 3, 2, and 1 categories. Group 5 stands for those which are *thought to be* great areas for the future, Group 4 includes strong favorites, Group 3 represents those fields which are in middle ground as far as current investment thinking is concerned, Group 2 includes less popular industries, and Group 1 contains those which are decidedly unpopular.

In listing these industries and their present ratings, I have posed some of the strongest positive and negative points per-

taining to them. Since space is limited and since I cannot
qualify as a specialist in every area, it behooves you to carry
the thought process one step further. Most important, however, is your understanding of the approach and your understanding of how to react to what has been presented. Under
any condition, your casual study of this will accomplish many
things for you, including:

1. You will know what current general investment thinking is.
2. You will develop a framework of reference about our
   economy.
3. You will know some important facts about the industries
   available for investment.
4. You will be engaging in practice of all-important "conceptual" thinking.
5. You will end up with a better "feel" about stocks and
   the market.

Most important, as indicated, is the carrying out of the
conceptual thinking, i.e., looking for the areas which are
either overpriced or overglamorized and those which are undervalued or unappreciated for what might be a glowing future. I strongly suggest you scan the ratings, become familiar
with the pros and cons, and recognize where each industry is
rated at this time. As mentioned, the industries are presented
in the order of their current rating category; for future reference, an index of the industries by alphabetical order is presented on page 223; and some concluding opinions of what
is most attractive and least attractive relative to the market is
discussed on page 224.

GROUP 5

Industry	Pertinent Positive Arguments	Important Negative Arguments
Drugs (Prescription)	Breakthroughs in major diseases and ailments. Expanding	Increased utilization of generic drugs (car- rying lower profit

Industry	Pertinent Positive Arguments	Important Negative Arguments
	usage by all age groups and by under-developed nations.	margins). Will Medicare bring heightened governmental interference?
Electronics	A necessary counterpart to trend toward automation, miniaturization, space exploration, etc. Countless exciting discoveries yet to come.	Rapid product obsolescence standard procedure. Necessary consolidation of many small companies existing (i.e., "shakeout" period ahead).
Office Equipment	Trend to automation and to growing need for labor-saving devices of all sorts.	Most exciting area (computers) requires huge outlays and has produced profits for only a few.
Photography	Ties in with expanding affluent society and increased leisure time. Film an expendable item—rapidly used up.	Obviously a "luxury" item, which might be affected if drastic recession set in.
Publishing	Tremendous push by government to educate the population means more texts, training books, etc. More-educated population from which to draw sales.	Better television programming would detract from reading time. Paperback field highly competitive; a difficult area in itself and a threat to hardcover sales. Publishing business highly competitive.

GROUP 4

Industry	Pertinent Positive Arguments	Important Negative Arguments
Airlines	Traffic-growth patterns very encourag-	A regulated industry which is bound to see

Industry	Pertinent Positive Arguments	Important Negative Arguments
	ing (and saturation point still low). Air freight in its infancy. New equipment offers interesting cost advantages.	heightened pressures for lower fares and more competition along routes. Transition to next-generation aircraft costly and may cause profit disruptions in short term.
Aluminum	Lightweight, durable metal, easy to fabricate. Still making inroads into other materials.	Question of when industry will reach relative maturity and be like other metals. Bound to be sensitive to business cycles.
Chemicals	Basic building blocks for so many items and thus so essential to economy. Not an easy entry business. Research can produce interesting new products.	Constant price competition. Ample capacity in most lines. Business has proved sensitive to economic fluctuations.
Drugs (Proprietary)	Classic example of firm price structure industry. Demand patterns strong. Low labor costs. Recession resistant.	Heavy advertising necessary. Breakthroughs not as dynamic as ethical side.
Electrical Equipment	Benefit from assured expansion of utilities. Large companies involved in nuclear energy and electronics items.	Long history of labor problems. Occasional price wars in heavy equipment and "white goods."
Oil	Per-capita energy consumption expand-	Risk of ownership in foreign lands. Possi-

Industry	Pertinent Positive Arguments	Important Negative Arguments
	ing. Companies possess huge assets which should always be converted to large profits.	bility of electric autos. Possibility that favorable tax treatment might be altered.
Radio-Television	Obvious demands for color TV and eventually for video recorders. Trend to more sets per family.	Very difficult industry under normal conditions. Low P/E multiple to be expected as color nears saturation.
Utilities	Offer an indispensable product in franchised areas. Demands increase consistently. No inventory problems.	Regulated by either state or federal commissions. Capital needs large. Growth slow (albeit steady).

GROUP 3

Industry	Pertinent Positive Arguments	Important Negative Arguments
Aerospace	Nation's future relies on strong military and defense. Companies also engaged in more-glamorous-than-aircraft areas (space technology, electronics).	Subject to changes in governmental spending, contract cancellations, etc. Profits are subject to renegotiation by government. High labor costs.
Aircraft (Private)	More and more individuals and companies flying their own planes. Improved takeoff and landing (i.e., helicopter) would open up vast markets. Only three major participants in field.	Business slowdowns could curtail purchases significantly. Chance that major aerospace firm(s) might enter this now-confined field.
Automobiles	More cars per family;	Strictly a durable

Industry	Pertinent Positive Arguments	Important Negative Arguments
Banking	more status of ownership of cars (part of affluent society). Burgeoning family-information figures ensure better markets. Money, never out of style, in constant demand. Money services will become more and more important.	good, purchase of which can be postponed. Sensitive to personal income, debt, savings. Style changes important. Industry having to bring salary standards up to compete with other businesses. Competition heightening.
Construction Equipment	Impetus from federal programs for schools, dams, highways. Underdeveloped countries now commencing huge programs.	Bound to be sensitive to business cycles (demands erratic). Cannot count on style changes to incite such purchases.
Containers	Obviously an essential business. Attractive packaging a necessary sales tool.	Possibility that more manufacturers will integrate and produce own materials and containers. Various products constantly competing with one another (paper *vs.* glass *vs.* plastics).
Cosmetics	Population increasingly aware of personal sanitation and adornment. Fits in with affluent society. Firm price structure and high return on invested capital.	Heavy advertising programs necessary and costs (from color TV) rising. Public can be fickle in product choices (certain ones, not all).
Foods	Stable business; not	Certain products non-

Industry	*Pertinent Positive Arguments*	*Important Negative Arguments*
	subject to wide fluctuations. Opportunity for interesting convenience foods and higher profitability with them.	differentiated (e.g. canned goods). Crop distortions and commodity prices can have effect on earnings. Heavy advertising required.
Insurance (Life)	Longer life expectancy and possibilities for disease breakthroughs beneficial. Needs for protection growing and better recognized. Premium schedules still favorable.	Group business, which is less profitable, growing. Numerous small companies entering the field. Accident and Health business difficult.
Paper	An expendable item, rapidly used up. Extensive timber reserves held considered a great asset.	Has not been well-disciplined price structure industry. Most paper nondifferentiated product. Ample capacity exists.
Retail Trade	Consumer a reliable spender. Industry just approaching automation techniques.	Competition from discount houses creates unhealthy condition. Hard to increase productivity of workers.
Rubber	More cars on road means more replacement demand. Major companies have strong retail outlets. Trend to higher-quality replacement tires provides greater profitability.	Original-equipment tires fluctuate with new-car sales and carry low margins. Has safety publicity caused high-end replacement to be overemphasized?

GROUP 2

Industry	Pertinent Positive Arguments	Important Negative Arguments
Building	Family-formation figures promise burgeoning demands. Emerging from period when money availability forced well-below-average construction. What will prefabrication techniques lead to?	Labor availability and rates a constant problem. Cyclical tendencies evidenced in the past. Most products have volatile price patterns.
Copper	World supplies controlled by small group. Basic to the attractive electrical-equipment outlook.	A world commodity which has had gyrations in past. Sensitive to business cycles and to pressures from other metals. Persistent labor troubles.
Farm Equipment	World food shortage means greater demands in future. Labor problems and farm sizes (larger) require more mechanization.	Sales sensitive to farm income. Public concern over subsidy programs.
Finance Companies	Credit buying now an accepted practice. Government and insurance programs make individuals better credit risks.	Relationship of consumer debt to income has grown to high proportions. More competition from banks, captive lending companies, credit unions.
Food Retailing	Frequently visited; sell essential items.	Is the country overstored? Typical low-

Industry	Pertinent Positive Arguments	Important Negative Arguments
	Chains still eliminating smaller, marginal stores. Alliance with other forms of retailing holds some potential.	margin business with all types of competitive devices.
Insurance (Fire and Casualty)	Investment income rising sharply. Getting greater rate relief. Now diversify into other (more profitable) financial areas.	Underwriting results very bad over the years. Inflation works against the industry. Rates are regulated, and lag in being granted a hindrance.
Machine Tools	Use of numeric-controlled (NC) tools opens up new vistas for those in this area. Constant need for businesses to modernize. NC tools have no secondhand market established yet— means firm pricing.	Sensitive to capital spending by businessmen. Wide swings in non-NC business will continue and be very cyclical.
Railroad Equipment	Vital need for improved equipment (rolling stock aged and need for more mechanization). Lease revenues lend stability.	Railroad cyclicality bound to affect equipment demands.
Railroads	Tremendous potentials from merger proposals. Possibility that unfair labor practices will diminish. Lever-	Inroads made by trucks, air freight, pipelines, etc. Very sensitive to cycle. Equipment needs

Industry	Pertinent Positive Arguments	Important Negative Arguments
	age from cost-savings huge.	huge. High labor factor.
Textiles	Industry in fewer (stronger) hands. Modernizing plants and getting greater productivity.	High labor costs and problems with rising minimum wage. Raw materials vary widely in price. Hard to control inventories.
Trucking	Short-haul business hard to replace by other means. Improved equipment on better highways means lower operating costs. Trend to less than carload lots favorable to industry.	Cyclically sensitive. High labor costs. Regulated industry. Long-haul business at disadvantage with new forms (piggyback, air freight). Asked to absorb heavier taxes emanating from highway programs.

GROUP 1

Industry	Pertinent Positive Arguments	Important Negative Arguments
Coal	Used by utilities (on long-term contracts). More company liquidations coming (worth more "dead" than alive).	Nuclear energy far more efficient. Steadily losing share of U.S. energy consumed.
Motion Pictures	Movie libraries represent tremendous assets —which should generate either large capital gains or consistent lease revenues over the years. Public willing to pay higher	Industry noted for extravagant overhead and lack of proper financial controls. Large risks taken in "spectacular"-type movies. Earnings bound to be somewhat

Industry	Pertinent Positive Arguments	Important Negative Arguments
	prices at box office for films. Signs that better financial management is taking hold in industry.	erratic, depending on new-picture success (or lack of same).
Savings and Loan	Higher interest rates to depositors have led to fast deposit growth. Many companies located in fastest-growing geographical regions (California in particular). Major companies now cleaning up excesses created in 1963–1966 period.	Banks becoming more competitive both for deposits and for real-estate commitments. Earning power of S&L's dependent in large part on riskier part of real-estate lending (i.e., construction loans). Question of management depth in most companies. Tax laws lead to low dividend payouts (companies would have to incur additional taxes to pay decent dividends to stockholders).
Steel	Industry spending two billion dollars annually on plant modernization and improvement. Break-even points being lowered consistently. Pricing has always been fairly well disciplined.	Steel obviously a metal at relative maturity. Demands bound to be tied to general economy—typical cyclical industry. High labor factor and history of labor problems.
Tobacco	Well-disciplined price structure. Always the possibility that some	Health hazards (both cancer and heart)— certainly indicate

Industry	Pertinent Positive Arguments	Important Negative Arguments
	anticancer development may be invented (i.e., filter development or similar). Companies diversifying into other consumer areas. Population age structure to industry's benefit.	strong evidence of linkage with smoking. Product lacks explosive growth even under normal (no-health-issue) conditions.

INDEX BY INDUSTRY

Industry Group	Group Rating
Machine Tools	2
Motion Pictures	1
Office Equipment	5
Oil	4
Paper	3
Photography	5
Publishing	5
Radio-Television	4
Railroad Equipment	2
Railroads	2
Retail Trade	3
Rubber	3
Savings and Loan	1
Steel	1
Textiles	2
Tobacco	1
Trucking	2
Utilities	4

CONCLUSIONS

Since the business of investing is one in which the most useful person is the one who takes a stand and places his ideas (and his "neck") on the block, I thought it might be helpful to carry the above one step further—by indicating which industries look too high or too low in their ratings at the time of this writing in late-1967.

To my way of thinking, the following groups carry too rich an evaluation by the investing community: airlines, aluminum, chemicals, electronics, publishing, and radio-television. In addition, I would consider a number of industries worthy of higher evaluation than shown, namely: building, cosmetics, proprietary drugs, life insurance, motion pictures, and utilities, with savings and loan and steel issues probably too low on more of a temporary nature.

Index

lected specialized fields of market, 15

Fad investments, how to avoid, 143–49, 210
Farm equipment, limited-choice area in, 70
Fear of loss, as factor in "stupidity of selling," 98
Fifth Avenue Coach Lines stock, gyrations of, in 1964, 151–53
Financial analysts, *see* Security analysts
"First stringers," investing in, 138, 141–42
Fixed-income securities: purchase of, in mergers, 61–62, 65–65; purchase of, in recovery situations, 62–65, 66; buying preferred stock as, 80–84
Flexibility, as important attribute in investing, 8–9
Food industry: and product differentiation, 30; convenience foods, as area of earnings growth certainty, 46
Foreign imports, as threat to metals industry, 106
Foresight, and the stock market, 3–12, 48, 58, 104, 117, 193, 197; Profit-Aid No. 1, 4, 9–10, 208–9; Zenith Radio stock, and color TV, 4–5, 10, 24; Brunswick and AMF stock, 6–8, 10, 21, 120, 157–58, 196–97; American Photocopy Equipment (Apeco) stock, 8–9, 10, 21; Industry-Rating Guide (Profit-Aid No. 2), 11–12, 15, 104, 209, 212–24; finding successful special-situation stocks, 21

Fortune, amassing of a, 95
Foundation stocks of the investor, 96, 101
"Fourth stringers," investing in, 138–42

General Motors stock, as general market criterion, 75–76
General Telephone-Sylvania Electric merger, 127
Georgia-Pacific's purchase of timber companies, 128
Glamour Rating of basic industries, *see* Industry Rating Guide
Glass, limited-choice area in basic research and new-product development, 70
Growth areas in the economy, investments in, 46
Growth companies: stock of, as sound investment, 34, 52; determining what price should be paid for growth, 34–41; importance of earnings growth, 40–41; in temporary downturns distinguished from out-and-out cyclical companies, 53; becoming holders, not sellers of, 100; productive research and development in, 175–78

Hanging on, philosophy of, in approach to investing, 97
Helene Curtis stock, grass-roots approach to, 119
Hewlett-Packard, and certainty in electronics industry, 45

About the Author

Claude N. Rosenberg, Jr., has had a uniquely successful career in the investment business, the basis of which has been his ability to uncover unusually profitable common stocks. His method of locating investments which might multiply ten, twenty, or thirty times over—and his ability to hang on for such unusual results—are all part of the *common sense* approach related in this book.

A native of San Francisco, where he is a general partner in the investment firm of J. Barth & Co., Mr. Rosenberg has both B.A. (Economics) and M.B.A. (Finance) degrees from Stanford University.